THE LODGE BOOK OF
DUTCH OVEN COOKING

J. WAYNE FEARS

Skyhorse Publishing

Skyhorse Publishing books may be purchased in bulk at special discounts for sales promotion, corporate gifts, fund-raising, or educational purposes. Special editions can also be created to specifications. For details, contact the Special Sales Department, Skyhorse Publishing, 307 West 36th Street, 11th Floor, New York, NY 10018 or info@skyhorsepublishing.com.

Skyhorse® and Skyhorse Publishing® are registered trademarks of Skyhorse Publishing, Inc.®, a Delaware corporation.

Visit our website at www.skyhorsepublishing.com.

10 9 8 7 6

Library of Congress Cataloging-in-Publication Data is available on file.

Cover design by Jane Sheppard
Cover photo credit: Abigail Gehring

Print ISBN: 978-1-63450-680-9
Ebook ISBN: 978-1-63450-860-5

Printed in China

To Sofee
She brings sunshine to every day, every situation.

CONTENTS

INTRODUCTION

If you saw an Internet or TV commercial advertising one cooking pot that would bake bread, steam vegetables, boil shrimp, fry eggs, stew wild game, and broil meats, chances are you might be interested. But what if the commercial went on to say that this nonstick pot could be used to cook a meal on your home stove, in your great room fireplace, on the patio, in a campfire at a state park, or on family camping trips? Plus, it's guaranteed to last through several generations of use. If you saw this commercial, your interest would probably be piqued and you would want to know a lot more about this magic pot.

The magic cooking pot that can do it all is the Dutch Oven.

THIS MAGIC POT IS THE DUTCH OVEN

There are a lot of different designs of cooking pots called Dutch Ovens. Some are designed for use with modern stoves. Others are cast-iron pots with long legs made famous by cooks on African safaris. (The real name for these pots is potjie and it dates back to the 1500s.) Yet others are cast iron pots with rounded bottoms designed to hang over open fires. And there are flat-bottomed cast-iron pots designed to sit on stoves or grills. These are often called kitchen Dutch Ovens.

Most outdoor cooks agree that the camp Dutch Oven is made from heavy cast iron and has a flat bottom that sits on three short legs protruding about 2 inches. It has a strong wire bail. The lid is made of the same heavy cast iron and has a small loop handle in the center. The rim of the lid is flanged so that hot coals will stay on the lid while cooking. Most people call these ovens camp Dutch Ovens to distinguish them from other Dutch Ovens. For the purpose of this book, these are the Dutch Ovens we will be talking about.

The Dutch Oven has been piquing cooks' interest for many centuries. It has been used in North America since the first settlers explored the Atlantic seaboard. Today, twenty-first-century cooks are finding the old-fashioned Dutch Oven just as much fun and just as valuable as the colonial cooks who depended on the pots to cook all their meals. While we don't have to stoop over a fireplace full of hot coals to cook a meal, cooks around the world are discovering the joy and good taste that comes with cooking in a Dutch Oven. Whether they are cooking for a party on their patio, cooking on a camping trip, or cooking in an emergency when the utilities are not working, the Dutch Oven produces great tasting food with a small amount of effort. Its use is also a fun family activity.

The Internet offers lots of Dutch Oven cooking advice and recipes—some good, some bad. Dutch Oven cook-offs have become popular gatherings for Dutch Oven fans and tourists alike. Dutch Oven enthusiasts have formed their own organization, the International Dutch Oven Society, to be a clearinghouse for Dutch Oven information and to foster interest in Dutch Oven cooking. For many people, Dutch Oven cooking has become part of their recreational pursuits, for others—guides, cowboys, outfitters, back-to-the-landers, and people living in

BELOW: A lot of pots, as shown, are called Dutch Ovens, but most Dutch Oven cooks consider the middle one the only real camp Dutch Oven.

Cow camp cooks, hunting guides, and many others use Dutch Ovens as part of their daily routines.

remote places—it is simply the way they cook hearty, wholesome meals daily. For preppers, this is a skill they learn and practice in the event we are thrown back to the 1700s by some horrible event. The camp Dutch Oven serves all well.

DON'T BE INTIMIDATED BY THE LEARNING PROCESS

It does take a little experience to learn to care for and successfully cook with Dutch Ovens, but once you get it down, it can be one of the most fun cooking experiences you can have. In fact, it is the ever-expanding learning process and caring for their cookware that most Dutch Oven cooks find the most interesting. Spend time around a group of experienced Dutch Oven cooks and you will hear a lot of conversation about seasoning techniques, the best coals to use, cooking in the wind, and always great new recipes. So don't let the learning process scare you away from what may be a lifetime of fun and exciting eating. For many, it is a hobby, and for a few it almost becomes a lifestyle.

HOW A QUALITY CAST IRON DUTCH OVEN IS MADE
CHAPTER ONE

According to Bob Kellermann at Lodge Manufacturing Company, the process for making cast iron hasn't really changed in six hundred years. It is the equipment, production speed, and quality of the final product that are enhanced through technology. Where there were once coke-fired cupolas to bring the iron to its molten state, now there is electric induction melting. It offers greater quality control and is significantly cleaner. In the past, each Dutch Oven was molded and poured by hand.

Today, automatic molding machines do it all. They are faster and yield more consistent product quality. Bob told me these facts when I visited the Lodge foundry in South Pittsburg, Tennessee, to see for myself how quality Dutch Ovens were made.

Many serious Dutch Oven cooks I have been around dream of a trip to Lodge to see how Dutch Ovens are made. I know of one Texas championship winning chuck-wagon cook who took his wife on a vacation to Tennessee just so they could visit the Dutch Oven manufacturing company.

While I was working on this book, Bob invited me to visit Lodge and go onto the foundry floor to watch Dutch Ovens being made. The trip gave me a whole new respect for quality Dutch Ovens, and I still wonder why they don't cost several hundred dollars apiece.

Just before my visit to Lodge, they had completed a huge expansion of the foundry. The expansion featured two 10-ton furnaces. The new Lodge melt center began operation in February 2014. In early November 2014, a new shot-blast cleaning machine began operation. Six days later, several other pieces of equipment, including a

New Dutch Ovens on their way to being packaged for shipping.

Every employee at Lodge acts as a quality-control inspector, checking each Dutch Oven as it is produced and packaged.

Disamatic pouring system, a Didion cleaning machine, and a new wash and spray and seasoning line were integrated into the production process.

The expansion altered the skyline of South Pittsburg with two new sand towers, standing 119 feet and 97 feet tall, used for the production and recycling of sand cast molds.

The expansion increases the company's production capacity by approximately 50 percent, with three production lines pouring, cleaning, and seasoning over 120 different Lodge Cast Iron Cookware items for domestic and international markets.

Here, in brief, are the steps that go into making a Lodge cast iron Dutch Oven:

1. First, a pattern of the Dutch Oven is made. This is the reverse image of the product with a gating system or small trough built into the mold. This will allow the molten metal to flow into the pattern to form the Dutch Oven.

2. The pattern is mounted on a molding machine that squeezes sand under extremely high pressure to form the mold. Each piece of cast iron cookware is formed in its own mold. High-quality sand is washed, dried, and mixed by grain fineness to Lodge specifications prior to delivery. Lodge tests the quality of the sand throughout production in a state-of-the-art lab.

3. Molten iron at 2500 degrees is poured into the cavity left by the pattern. Iron melts at approximately 2000 degrees, but Lodge heats it an additional 800 degrees for maximum fluidity and smooth pouring. The iron used must meet stringent Lodge standards. Today, through an amazing piece of equipment called a spectrometer, Lodge is able to test the elemental makeup of the iron and monitor for consistency during production.

4. After the metal cools and solidifies to form a casting, it is mechanically removed from the sand.

5. The sand used to make the casting is recycled—reduced to grain size, re-coated with clay and water, and reintroduced to the molding machine to be used again. The metal poured into the cavity is called gating, and it is recycled into the system mentioned above. Gating is recycled back to the furnace. Roughly 110 tons of recycled sand and 6 tons of iron are used each hour of production.

Bob Kellermann, left, explains to the author how Lodge Dutch Ovens are preseasoned.

6. The complete removal of sand baked on a casting at 2500 degrees takes some force. To clean cast iron cookware, abrasive steel shot is catapulted all over each item.
7. Then rough edges from the casting process are ground smooth.
8. The Dutch Oven enters an eight-minute metal media wash that deburrs any sharp edges left over from grinding.
9. The raw cast iron Dutch Oven is then sprayed with a soy-based vegetable oil, and the oil is baked onto the metal at a very high temperature, turning the pot from gray to a black patina. Now it is seasoned.
10. Finally, the Dutch Oven is sent to packaging, segregated from other types of products, labeled, packaged, loaded on pallets, and added to inventory.

One of the things that impressed me the most during my visit was that during every step of the process, every employee acts as a quality-control inspector. If imperfections or slight blemishes are found, the product is removed from the line.

As I said in the beginning, I don't see why these quality-made ovens aren't priced at several hundred dollars. I am just glad that, thanks to modern, highly efficient machinery and management, quality Dutch Ovens are still affordable and long lasting.

Lodge makes cast iron Dutch Ovens in sizes from 5 inches up to 14 inches, both shallow and deep. Their standard 6-inch oven is 3 inches deep, the 8-inch oven is 3 inches deep, the 10-inch oven is 3½ inches deep, the 12-inch oven is 3¾ inches deep, and the 14-inch oven is 3¾ inches deep. Their deep (or meat) Dutch Ovens are

Molten iron is poured into the transfer ladle.

roomier: the 10-inch Dutch Oven is 4 inches deep, the 12-inch is 5 inches deep, and the 14-inch is 5 inches deep.

Use the chart on page 15 to select which size Dutch Oven you will want based on the amount of food you will be cooking and the number of people you will serve. Keep in mind that most experienced Dutch Oven cooks never try to cook an entire meal with one oven. They use several ovens in various sizes to cook several dishes at one time.

BELOW: To determine the size of a Dutch Oven, measure across the top of the pot. A 12-inch oven is called a #12.

SELECTING A DUTCH OVEN

Oven size	Oven capacity	Persons served	Weight (pounds)
6-INCH	1 QUART	1	5
8-INCH	2 QUARTS	2–4	11
10-INCH	4 QUARTS	4–7	13
10-INCH	5 QUARTS	8–10	14
12-INCH	6 QUARTS	12–14	20
12-INCH DEEP	8 QUARTS	16–20	21
14-INCH	8 QUARTS	16–20	26
14-INCH DEEP	10 QUARTS	22–28	27
16-INCH	10 QUARTS	22–28	35

Courtesy of Lodge Manufacturing Company.

THE BENEFITS OF CAST IRON DUTCH OVENS
CHAPTER TWO

Cast iron Dutch Ovens are steeped in history and tradition, and a large number of Dutch Oven cooks prefer the advantages of cast iron. Here are the benefits most often given.

Along with the many advantages of cooking with cast iron Dutch Ovens, they also provide nutritional benefits.

Long lasting:

Cast iron Dutch Ovens are famous for lasting generations and becoming family heirlooms. Many around today are well over one hundred years old. During the pioneering days of early America, the family cast iron Dutch Oven was valuable enough to be included in wills. John Rutledge, writing in his excellent book, *Dutch Ovens Chronicled*, tells of Mary Washington, mother of General George Washington, wanting to be certain her cast iron vessels were cared for. In her will, dated May 20, 1788, she provided that one half of her "iron kitchen furniture" would go to a grandson, Fielding Lewis, and the other half would go to a granddaughter, Betty Carter. Rutledge states, "Surely there were several Dutch Ovens among her iron kitchen furniture." Most Dutch Oven cooks will be quick to tell you, the older a cast iron oven gets, the better it cooks.

Distributes heat evenly:

While cast iron ovens take a little longer to heat up, the heat is distributed evenly, resulting in fewer "hot spots" and giving ideal cooking conditions. If your food burns, the oven is too hot. Less heat is needed with cast iron.

Retains heat:

Cast iron ovens, once heated to a desired temperature, are easier than aluminum to keep at that temperature. Cast iron ovens require less fuel and time refueling.

Heavy lid seals in steam:

The heavy, tight-fitting lid of a cast iron Dutch Oven helps hold steam in, so the oven acts as a pressure cooker and helps keep food tender and moist.

Nutritional benefits:

According to many Dutch Oven experts, cooking in cast iron Dutch Ovens is healthy, as cast iron cookware imparts a significant amount of dietary iron to your food, which is absorbed by the body.

Tolerates higher heat:

No Dutch Oven should be subjected to high temperatures, but on occasion it does happen, When it does, the cast iron oven stands a good chance of surviving the event because cast iron melts at around 2200 degrees F. Wind-blown coals and campfires can generate temperatures in those ranges. Overall, a cast iron heats more slowly so it's less prone to temperature flare-ups and food is better protected from burning.

Cast iron cookware stands the test of time, with most products lasting a century or longer.

CHAPTER THREE

Breads and Dutch Ovens go together like glove and hand. Dutch Ovens are easy to bake in and make bread baking a snap, even in the backcountry. It is not only ideal for baking bread you make from scratch, but for baking store-bought bread as well.

An entire meal of bread, main course, and dessert can be cooked at one time.

Since Dutch Ovens hold heat so well, don't forget that when baking bread you need to remove the bread as soon as you take the oven from the coals. Not doing this can result in wet bread, as the water condensation on the lid will drip down on the bread as the oven cools.

An entire book, no, an entire series of books, could be written giving bread recipes that could be cooked in the Dutch Oven. For this chapter, I have selected basic breads that every Dutch Oven cook should know. And since most Dutch Oven cooks have an interest in history, several of these recipes have a tie with history.

The first will be bannock, known as bread of the wilderness. This is an easy and simple bread that was handed down to us by history and is a good bread for the beginning cook.

Another is hoecake, very similar in its historic origin and simple to cook. The chief difference is the hoecake is not baked; it is cooked on the inverted lid of a Dutch Oven.

TATER KNOB HOECAKE

Hoecake has many names. Many know it as pan bread, skillet bread, or corn pone. This bread is said to have been first used by African-American slaves prior to the War Between the States. It is said it was the nearest thing Southern troops, on short rations, had to use as bread. After the war, it was a staple among displaced settlers, and it found its way from there to the western frontier and on to the gold fields of Alaska and the Yukon.

It is simple to make, and those of us who have eaten it for long periods of time like it. It is usually fried on the inverted Dutch Oven lid but it can be cooked in the oven as well.

Portions: 2
Dutch Oven: Any size

INGREDIENTS

1 cup self-rising cornmeal
dash of salt
1 egg
enough buttermilk to make a paste

METHOD

1. Heat the Dutch Oven lid.

2. Put a small amount of cooking oil into the lid.

3. Combine the cornmeal, salt, egg and buttermilk to create a paste.

4. Once the oil is hot, pour in the hoecake paste. Let it brown on the bottom before turning.

5. It's done with the top is brown.

BANNOCK

Far up in the north country of North America, the seventeenth-century French-Canadian voyagers opened up the wilderness from the Great Lakes to northwest Canada. These great canoeists traveled vast distances on light rations. One of their main staples was bannock, a simple bread of Scottish descent. Bannock has been the bread of the wilderness traveler for centuries in the cold north country and is still very popular among those who spend their time in the backcountry.

Bannock is usually cooked in a Dutch Oven as a loaf, but you can roll it out and make biscuits.

An interesting side note: this bannock mix can be used for dishes other than bread. I have used it as a base for making pancakes, dumplings, pie crust, batter for fish, and as a base for cakes and rolls. The settler or expedition that had a supply of bannock mix could create a variety of dishes.

Portions: 2
Dutch Oven: 10-inch

INGREDIENTS

1 cup all-purpose flour
2 level teaspoons double-acting
  baking powder
½ teaspoon salt
2 teaspoons powdered skim milk
water

METHOD

1. Preheat the Dutch Oven.

2. Sift together the dry ingredients, then stir in enough water to make moist but firm dough.

3. Place the dough on a floured board and knead, handling the dough as little as possible.

4. Flatten the dough into a disk and place it in the preheated Dutch Oven.

5. Bake until golden brown.

SOUTHERN BISCUITS & COUNTRY GRAVY

This is a favorite quick-to-make biscuit recipe that has been dubbed Southern Biscuits. When combined with Pioneer Brand Country Gravy mix, just as quick to make, it makes a great breakfast basic. Combine them with sausage and grits or hash browns, perhaps some homemade strawberry jelly, and you have a breakfast fit for a king.

Portions: 2
Dutch Oven: 10-inch

INGREDIENTS

2 cups self-rising flour
¼ cup vegetable shortening
⅔–¾ cups buttermilk

METHOD

1. Preheat the Dutch Oven.

2. Spray a baking pan with nonstick cooking spray.

3. Put the flour into a large bowl. Cut in shortening with a knife until crumbs are the size of peas. Using a fork, blend in just enough milk so the dough leaves the sides of the bowl.

4. Turn out the dough onto a lightly floured surface. Knead gently two to three times. Roll the dough to a ½ inch thickness. Cut the dough using a floured 2-inch biscuit cutter. Place the biscuits in the cake pan with the sides touching.

5. Place the cake pan in the Dutch Oven.

6. Bake until golden brown.

COUNTRY GRAVY

INGREDIENTS

1 package Pioneer Brand
   Country Gravy mix
2 cups water

METHOD

1. Bring 1½ cups of water to a rolling boil.

2. Blend Country Gravy mix with ½ cup cool water. Whisk until it's free of lumps.

3. Pour the gravy mix blend into the boiling water. Stir vigorously with a whisk until thickened. Remove from heat.

4. Serve over biscuits.

COUNTRY DUTCH CORNBREAD

I have always loved cornbread and have said that the only way cornbread isn't good is when it's burned. Well, when I first started cooking cornbread in a Dutch Oven I burned a lot. Many cornbread recipes are not very forgiving when small mistakes are made in a hot oven. My family kept working with cornbread recipes until we came up with this one designed for Dutch Oven cooking.

Don't settle for just one cornbread recipe, as it is amazing what you can do with a basic cornbread mix. I have been a judge at the National Cornbread Championship Cook-Off and have tasted many outstanding one-pot meals that were started with cornbread. This simple recipe should get you off to a good start.

Portions: 8
Dutch Oven: 12-inch

INGREDIENTS

2 cups Martha White Self-Rising
　　Buttermilk Corn Meal Mix
⅓ cups milk
¼ cup oil or melted shortening
1 egg, beaten
dash of salt

METHOD

1. Preheat the Dutch Oven.

2. Grease a 9-inch round pan.

3. In a bowl, combine all ingredients, mixing well. Pour batter into the greased pan.

4. Place the pan on a cake rack inside your Dutch Oven.

5. Bake until golden brown.

SOURDOUGH BISCUITS

Dutch Ovens and sourdough bread go together, if for no other reason than they are so tied together in the history of western America exploration. Chances were good, and still are, that if you found an outfitter, miner, homesteader, or trapper they had/have a cast iron Dutch Oven and a jar of sourdough starter at camp. Sourdough bread is just as good today as it was for the miners of Alaska in the late 1890s or the cowboys who drove cattle to the railheads in the late 1800s and early 1900s. For this reason, we are including a starter recipe and a basic sourdough bread recipe.

You cannot have sourdough bread, pancakes, muffins, or cakes without having a starter. The starter can be stored in a clay pot or glass jar in the refrigerator for use at a later time. I got this starter recipe from the Alaskan Cooperative Extension Service many years ago.

Portions: 6–8
Dutch Oven: 10-inch

SOURDOUGH STARTER

INGREDIENTS

2 cups all-purpose flour
2 cups warm water
1 package dry yeast

METHOD

1. Combine all ingredients in a plastic bowl.
2. Place the bowl in a warm location overnight.
3. In the morning, put ½ cup of the starter in a scalded pint jar. Cover the jar and store in the refrigerator for future use.
4. The remaining batter, called sponge, can be used immediately to make sourdough bread.

SOURDOUGH BISCUITS

INGREDIENTS

2 cups sourdough starter
2 cups all-purpose flour, sifted
2 tablespoons Crisco shortening
2 teaspoons baking powder
1 tablespoon sugar
½ teaspoon salt
½ stick butter

METHOD

1. Preheat the Dutch Oven.
2. Put the flour in a large mixing bowl and create a well in the center.
3. Add the sourdough starter.
4. Add the baking powder, sugar, and salt. Next, cut in the Crisco.
5. Mix the dough to form a soft ball.
6. Break off walnut-sized pieces of dough and roll them into balls. Place the balls into a greased 9-inch aluminum pan so the sides are touching.
7. Baste the tops with melted butter.
8. Cover the pan and place it in a warm spot for 10 minutes so the dough will rise.
9. Place the pan inside the Dutch Oven and bake until golden brown.

Serve hot. Sourdough biscuits can become very firm when cold. Reheated, they become soft again. Leftover sourdough biscuits are great for making bread pudding.

APPLESAUCE BREAD

Simple breads are sometimes the best. This bread is easy to prepare and bake, and is just as delicious at camp or backyard cookouts. Make this bread ahead and freeze to take on future outings.

Portions: 4
Dutch Oven: 10-inch

INGREDIENTS

½ cup milk
2 cups flour
1 yeast packet
¼ cup applesauce

METHOD

1. Heat the milk until warm, then pour it into a mixing bowl.

2. Add the flour, yeast, and applesauce. Mix to combine.

3. Let the dough rise for 30 minutes.

4. Form the dough into a loaf.

5. Put the loaf in an aluminum liner pan, then place it in the Dutch Oven.

6. Bake until golden brown.

MAIN DISHES
CHAPTER FOUR

Every Dutch Oven cook has a main dish favorite they like to cook in their ovens. I differ only that I have a lot of favorite main dishes. I think fish baked in Dutch Ovens tastes better than fish prepared any other way. Wild game and the black pot seem to be made for each other. Chicken is great for Dutch Oven cooking, as it can be cooked so many good ways and is forgiving to mistakes made by new cooks.

The main dish and a side dish being cooked at the same time in a New Mexico hunting camp.

Many of my favorite dishes are one-pot dishes, great for the owner of just one oven. Other main dishes can be part of a great feast and cooked with other Dutch Oven favorites using the stack-cooking technique. Many cooks use soups, stews, and chili as side dishes, but in many of the camps and patios where I cook, these delicious dishes are hearty enough to stand alone as a main dish. The following Brunswick Stew, Santa Fe Soup, Zesty Surprise Chili, and my favorite stew, Sara's Stew, are such dishes.

The game bird hunter will find Big Woods Chicken a favorite way to prepare waterfowl and upland game birds. Non-hunters will find that it will become a popular chicken recipe. And if you like Cornish game hens, then there is a recipe for you.

Meat lovers will fall in love with the Longhunters Meatloaf, Tender Roast, Reuben Casserole, and Pork & White Vegetables. These are easy recipes to follow and almost foolproof for the inexperienced Dutch Oven cook. If you want to get away from fried fish, try the Northrop Halibut Steaks or French Baked Salmon—easy to prepare and no frying.

For those who have a bean hole (see chapter 10), the Roast Beef and Veggies is an ideal slow–cooked meal that can be placed in the bean hole early in the morning to have dinner ready in the evening.

The Dutch Oven can be used as a stew pot as well, and Sara's Beef Stew is one of the best examples of just how good a meal the Dutch Oven can make hanging over an open fire from a tripod.

The Mountain Man Breakfast has been around for many years and is a favorite among Dutch Oven chefs. While it is best known as a breakfast one-pot meal, I have served it many times for dinner and it was a hit for those who ate it.

BRUNSWICK STEW

The Brunswick Stew recipe I like is thought to be more than two hundred years old. It was found in journals dating back to the 1700s, and it has been said that such notables as Patrick Henry and Alexander Hamilton ate this stew at Cold Spring Club and City Tavern. It has been recorded that Dr. Creed Haskins cooked this first stew in a Dutch Oven in Brunswick, Virginia, and it became traditional at cockfights, rifle matches, and political rallies.

I have slightly changed the original recipe since it called for two gray squirrels cut up into pieces and some of the people I cook for do not like squirrel. Chicken or turkey will do just as well.

Portions: 8
Dutch Oven: 12-inch

INGREDIENTS

3 cups precooked shredded turkey
4 cups water
2 potatoes, diced
1 onion, diced
1 can corn
1 cup lima beans
1½ teaspoons salt
½ teaspoon pepper
1 can tomatoes
1 teaspoon sugar
¼ cup butter
½ teaspoon turmeric
¼ cup vinegar
½ teaspoon hot sauce

METHOD

1. Combine the turkey, water, potatoes, onion, corn, lima beans, salt, and pepper, in the Dutch Oven.

2. Cook 30 minutes.

3. Add the tomatoes, sugar, butter, turmeric, vinegar, and hot sauce

4. Cook on low heat until all ingredients are done and the flavors blended.

5. Clean the Dutch Oven as soon as possible.

SANTA FE SOUP

Here is a good soup for cold days. It makes a great one-pot meal when served with Country Dutch Cornbread or Tater Knob Hoecake.

Portions: 12+
Dutch Oven: 12-inch, Deep

INGREDIENTS

2 pounds ground turkey or beef
1 medium onion, diced
2 packages ranch dressing mix
2 packages taco seasoning mix
2 cups water
16 ounces kidney beans
16 ounces pinto beans
16 ounces black beans
1 frozen bag white shoe peg corn
1 can Rotel tomatoes

Note: This recipe makes a lot and will keep in the refrigerator for a week or longer. It freezes well and can be served as soup or topping on chips with salsa and sour cream, depending on how much water you add.

METHOD

1. Brown the meat in a skillet, then add the onions and cook 5 more minutes.

2. Place in a 3-inch-deep aluminum pan.

3. Add the ranch dressing mix and taco seasoning.

4. Next, add the water.

5. Add the beans, shoe peg corn, and tomatoes.

6. Place in the Dutch Oven and simmer until done.

ZESTY SURPRISE CHILI

Thanks to the numerous chili cook-offs held annually around the country, there are scores of good chili recipes. This recipe came from a friend, and it cooks up good in a Dutch Oven.

Portions: 6
Dutch Oven: 12-inch

INGREDIENTS

1 pound ground meat of choice, we used nilgai
1 tablespoon oil
1 whole onion, chopped
1 whole bell pepper, chopped
1 package French's Chili-O seasoning mix
1 can Del Monte petite cut tomatoes with zesty jalapeños
2 cans Del Monte diced tomatoes with basil, garlic, and oregano
1 tablespoon chili powder
2 cans kidney beans, drained
1 can mushrooms

METHOD

1. In a Dutch Oven, brown ground meat in oil.

2. Add the onion and bell pepper and cook until tender. Drain.

3. Add the Chili-O mix, tomatoes, and chili powder. Mix well.

4. Add the chili beans

5. Add the mushrooms.

6. Cook until the flavors blend.

7. Clean the Dutch Oven as soon as possible.

BIG WOODS CHICKEN

Here is a versatile recipe that I first learned how to cook in North Dakota where the bird was snow goose. Later I tried the recipe in Maine on ruffed grouse. The results were so good, I tried it on chicken—something that was in supply year-round—and it turned out extremely good. So, if you have game birds use them, or you can just run out and buy a chicken. They are all good.

Portions: 4
Dutch Oven: 12-inch, Deep

INGREDIENTS

½ cup sweet onion, diced
½ cup red wine
½ cup cream of mushroom soup
½ cup cream of onion soup
½ cup cream of chicken soup
½ cup sliced mushrooms
1 small whole chicken

METHOD

1. Sauté the diced onion in a Dutch Oven.

2. Combine the onion, wine, soups, and mushrooms in a bowl.

3. Place the onion in the bottom of a round, 3-inch-deep aluminum pan. Then, place the chicken in the pan and pour the mixture over it.

4. Place the pan in a Dutch Oven and cook until the chicken reaches an internal temperature of 165 degrees.

5. This chicken is best served over rice. Pour the broth over the chicken and rice.

FRENCH BAKED SALMON

I love salmon fishing and salmon eating. One fall while on New York's famous Salmon River, Dutch Oven chef Ken French shared this recipe with me. The mayo coating forms a crust on the salmon steak, sealing in the juices and flavor. This dish will convert a non-Dutch Oven cook into a full devotee.

Portions: 2
Dutch Oven: 10-inch

INGREDIENTS

¼ cup mayonnaise
1 pound salmon steak
½ teaspoon Season All seasoning mix
1 teaspoon Cavender's Greek
   Seasoning

METHOD

1. Smear a layer of mayonnaise on all sides of the salmon steak.

2. Combine the two seasonings in a bowl, then sprinkle onto the steak.

3. Put a cake rack inside a 9-inch cake pan. Place the steak on top of the rack.

4. Place the cake pan on a trivet inside a 10-inch Dutch Oven.

5. Bake until golden brown

LONGHUNTER MEATLOAF

This is a simple meatloaf recipe that works well with almost any type of lean ground meat. I prefer venison, elk, caribou, or moose, but beef will do. When cooked in a loaf pan in the Dutch Oven, cleaning up is quick and easy.

Portions: 4–5
Dutch Oven: 12-inch

INGREDIENTS

⅔ cup dry breadcrumbs
1 cup milk
1½ pounds ground meat
2 eggs, beaten
¼ cup onion, grated
1 teaspoon salt
dash of pepper
½ teaspoon sage
½ teaspoon thyme
½ teaspoon rosemary
Catsup or favorite sauce for topping

METHOD

1. In large bowl, soak the breadcrumbs in milk.

2. Add meat, eggs, onion, seasonings, and herbs. Combine well.

3. Form the mixture into a loaf and place in a nonstick or cast iron 8½ x 4½ x 2½-inch loaf pan.

4. Spread ketchup or your favorite sauce over the top.

5. Place the loaf pan on a cake rack inside the Dutch Oven.

6. Bake until the internal temperature reaches 160 degrees.

REUBEN CASSEROLE WITH CORNBREAD

Several years ago, I had the honor of judging the National Cornbread Cook-Off held annually in South Pittsburg, Tennessee. It was a tight contest and all the finalists brought in outstanding one-pot dishes made with cornbread bases. It wasn't until the judges bit into Janice Carver's Reuben Casserole that we had a winner. It was one of the best cornbread casseroles any of us had ever tasted. She walked away with the National Championship. Here is Carver's recipe, which I cook in my Dutch Oven.

Portions: 6
Dutch Oven: 14-inch, Deep

INGREDIENTS

FILLING

2 (10-ounce) cans sauerkraut, drained
2 medium tomatoes, thinly sliced
⅓ cup Thousand Island dressing
1 (2¼-ounce) can sliced black olives, drained
6 ounces sliced corned beef, shredded
1½ cups (6 ounces) shredded Swiss cheese

CORNBREAD MIXTURE

1 large egg
1 cup buttermilk
⅓ cup milk
3 tablespoons vegetable oil
1 cup Martha White Self-Rising White Corn Meal Mix
⅓ cup Martha White Self-Rising Flour
1 tablespoon sugar

MUSTARD SAUCE *(optional)*

½ cup mayonnaise
½ cup prepared mustard
1 teaspoon onion, finely chopped

METHOD

1. Preheat the Dutch Oven.

2. Layer the sauerkraut, tomatoes, salad dressing, olives, and corned beef in a 10-inch by 3-inch-deep, aluminum pan. Top with the cheese. Set aside.

3. Make the crust: beat the egg in a medium bowl. Whisk in the buttermilk, milk, and oil. Mix well. Add the corn meal mix, flour, and sugar. Stir until smooth. Pour the batter evenly over the filling in the aluminum pan.

4. Place in a Dutch Oven and bake until golden brown.

5. Make the mustard sauce: combine the mayonnaise, mustard, and onion in a small bowl and stir to blend.

6. Cut the casserole into wedges and serve with the mustard sauce.

NORTHROP HALIBUT STEAKS

Medrick and Diane Northrop are good friends who lived for years in Alaska. Each year, they would go off-shore fishing and get their own halibut steaks. Since Medrick is one of the best Dutch Oven cooks I have ever shared a fire with, I asked him to give me his best Dutch Oven halibut recipe. It's just as good as he said it was.

Portions: 4–5
Dutch Oven: 10-inch

INGREDIENTS

½ cup flour
½ cup cornmeal
½ tsp. rosemary
½ tsp. garlic salt
½ tsp. black pepper
½ tsp. mustard
½ cup milk
1 ½ pounds halibut steaks, enough
   to cover the bottom of the Dutch
   Oven or cake pan
1 onion, thinly sliced (optional)
½ stick butter
paprika
chives or green onion tops, chopped
8 oz. Parmesan cheese, grated
lemon wedges

METHOD

1. Grease the bottom and sides of a cake pan or Dutch Oven.

2. Combine the flour, cornmeal, and seasonings in a bowl.

3. Dip the halibut in milk, then dredge it in the flour and cornmeal mixture.

4. Arrange the halibut, skin side down, so it completely covers the bottom of the Dutch Oven or cake pan.

5. Cover the halibut with the onion slices, then cover with butter cut into pieces.

6. Sprinkle with paprika and/or chives.

7. Cover with the Parmesan cheese.

8. Bake until golden brown. Halibut should flake easily.

9. Garnish with lemon wedges and serve.

PORK & WHITE VEGETABLES

This is a dish that came from Germany and serves as a one-pot meal.

Portions: 6
Dutch Oven: 12-inch

INGREDIENTS

3 cups onions, sliced
3 cups potatoes, thinly sliced
3 cups cabbage, sliced
1 can shredded sauerkraut, drained
5 links pork, grilled

METHOD

1. Layer the onions on the bottom of the Dutch Oven.

2. Place the potatoes in a layer on top of the onions.

3. Layer the sliced cabbage on top of the potatoes.

4. Add salt and pepper to taste.

5. Layer the sauerkraut on top of the cabbage.

6. Place the grilled meat on top.

7. Cook until the potatoes slices are done.

TENDER ROAST

I discovered this recipe when I owned hunting lodges. I often had clients that complained of venison roast being tough. Using my Dutch Ovens, I tried different recipes for roast until I found this one. It can take a less-than-tender roast, whether it be venison or beef, and make it tender.

Portions: 4–5
Dutch Oven: 10-inch, Deep

INGREDIENTS

4 pounds venison or beef roast
1 cup hot water
1 package dry onion soup mix
1 tablespoon Worcestershire sauce

METHOD

1. Place the roast on a trivet inside the Dutch Oven.

2. Combine hot water and the soup mix, using just enough water to make a thick paste.

3. Brush the paste over the roast.

4. Sprinkle Worcestershire sauce over the roast.

5. Put 1 cup of water in the Dutch Oven.

6. Bake until the roast reaches an internal temperature of 145 degrees.

7. Remove the roast immediately from the Dutch Oven and serve hot.

SARA'S BEEF STEW

Here is a great example of how you can use your Dutch Oven as a cook pot over a campfire, hanging from a tripod over a campfire, or on a grill over an open fire. This beef stew is one of the best I have ever eaten. It is the creation of Sara Graves, wife of chuckwagon/Dutch Oven master chef Roger Graves. It differs from most stew recipes where the ingredients are simply dumped into a pot of water and cooked. This one has a few extra steps that result in one of the best stews ever.

Portions: 6–8
Dutch Oven: Two 12-inch, Deep

INGREDIENTS

1 package Adolph's Beef Stew Mix
2 tablespoons vegetable oil
3 pounds beef round, cut into 1-inch
  cubes
1 cup flour
1 package McCormick's Beef Stew
  Seasoning
1 package McCormick's Brown Gravy
  Mix
6 large Irish potatoes, cubed
1 cup carrots, peeled and sliced

Note from Sara: I have made this recipe using each of the stew mixes separately. Neither one gave me the desired flavor results. Each had flavors I liked, so I combined them to get the taste I wanted. Adding the gravy just complements the rich and satisfying flavor of the finished product.

METHOD

1. Put 3 quarts of water in a Dutch Oven over medium-high heat.

2. Stir Adolph's Beef Stew Mix into 2 cups of warm water, then pour into the Dutch Oven.

3. While that cooks, heat the oil in a skillet over medium heat. Coat the cubed meat with flour then brown on all sides.

4. Add the meat to the Dutch Oven and stir. Cover, reduce heat to low, and cook for 2 hours, stirring every 20–30 minutes to prevent meat from sticking to the bottom.

5. Stir the McCormick's Beef Stew Seasoning Mix into 2 cups of warm water. Add to the Dutch Oven mixture and stir well.

6. Combine the gravy mix and 2 cups of warm water. Add to the Dutch Oven and stir.

7. While the stew continues to cook on low heat, peel and cut the potatoes and carrots. Bring water to a boil in two pots, then add the vegetables. Let them cook until they can be easily pierced with a fork. Remove and drain. (Cooking the vegetables separately has proven to keep them more tender.)

8. Add the vegetables to the Dutch Oven and stir.

CORNISH GAME HENS

Here is one of the easiest main dishes I have ever cooked. Serve with baked apples and you have a meal everyone will like.

Portions: 4
Dutch Oven: 12-inch

INGREDIENTS

4 Cornish game hens
salt and pepper to taste
½ stick butter, melted
¼ cup orange juice
¼ cup honey

METHOD

1. Preheat the Dutch Oven.

2. Place hens on a rack in a 9-inch baking pan.

3. Sprinkle hens with salt and pepper.

4. In a small bowl, combine the butter, orange juice, and honey. Spoon over the hens.

5. Place in a Dutch Oven and bake until a meat thermometer registers 165 degrees and juices run clear.

6. Baste every 15 minutes during cooking.

7. Serve hens on a bed of brown rice.

SAUCE

INGREDIENTS

½ cup orange juice
2 tablespoons honey
½ teaspoon cider vinegar
1 tablespoon cornstarch
1 tablespoon cold water

METHOD

1. In a small saucepan, combine the orange juice, honey, and vinegar. Combine the cornstarch and water until smooth, then stir into the orange juice mixture.

2. Bring to a boil; cook and stir for 1 minute or until thickened.

3. Serve with the hens.

MOUNTAIN MAN BREAKFAST

This is a favorite around campfires all across America. It can be cooked as a breakfast one-pot meal, a hot lunch, or served up with Southern Biscuits and Country Gravy for an evening feast.

Portions: 4
Dutch Oven: 10-inch

INGREDIENTS

1 pound country sausage
1 pound frozen hash brown potatoes
4 eggs, beaten with ⅛ cup water
1 cup sharp cheddar cheese, shredded

METHOD

1. Fry and crumble the sausage in a 10-inch Dutch Oven.

2. Remove sausage and drain on a paper towel.

3. Over the sausage grease in the Dutch Oven, spread and brown the hash brown potatoes.

4. Place the cooked sausage over the cooked hash browns.

5. Pour the eggs over the hash browns and sausage.

6. Sprinkle cheese over the top of the mixture.

7. Bake until the eggs are cooked.

BEAN HOLE POT ROAST AND VEGGIES

Not having a slow cooker in camp is no reason not to have the advantage of slow, all-day cooking. All you have to do is to build a bean hole (see chapter 10) and you have the oldest slow cooker in America. One of the easiest ways to have a hot one-pot meal waiting for you after a day of fishing, hunting, or exploring is to cook a pot roast and veggies in the bean hole using your Dutch Oven.

Start by building a hot fire in the bean hole and let it burn for about one hour. While the bean hole is heating up, use this recipe to prepare supper. Place the Dutch Oven with the ingredients into the hot hole, cover with hot coals, and seal the bean hole shut. Come back in 8 to 10 hours and you have a hot meal waiting to be uncovered.

Portions: 4
Dutch Oven: 12-inch, Deep

INGREDIENTS

4 pounds chuck roast
salt and pepper to taste
1 packet dry onion soup mix
3 medium sweet onions, cut into
   quarters
3 russet potatoes, peeled and cut into
   1-inch cubes
2 cups baby carrots
1 cup beef broth
1 cup water

METHOD

1. Season the roast with salt and pepper, then place on a trivet inside the Dutch Oven.

2. Sprinkle the soup mix over the roast.

3. Add the onions, potatoes, and carrots to the pot.

4. Next, add the beef broth and water.

5. Seal the pot with aluminum foil, leaving enough slack so the lid still fits snugly.

6. Place the lid on the pot and seal it in place with aluminum foil.

7. Lower the Dutch Oven into the bean hole and cover the lid with hot ashes.

8. Place the top on the bean hole and cover with dirt.

9. Return in 8 to 10 hours and uncover your hot pot roast dinner.

BASE CAMP ONE-POT CHICKEN DINNER

If you need to serve dinner for a large group, this one-pot chicken meal gets the job done, and everyone will be asking you for the recipe.

Portions: 10–12
Dutch Oven: 14-inch, Deep

INGREDIENTS

5 pounds chicken breast, cubed
2 medium yellow sweet onions, chopped
2 green peppers, chopped
1 large yellow squash, cubed
1 (19-ounce) can enchilada sauce
25 small corn tortillas
2 pounds shredded sharp cheddar cheese
1 (16-ounce) can pinto beans
1 (16-ounce) can corn
3 boxes Jiffy Cornbread Mix
3 eggs
1 cup milk

METHOD

1. Sauté the chicken, onions, green peppers, and squash.

2. In the Dutch Oven, layer the enchilada sauce, tortillas, cheese, beans, corn, and the cooked chicken and veggies mixture.

3. Mix the cornbread according to the instructions on the box and spread over the top.

4. Bake until the cornbread is golden brown.

SIDE DISHES
CHAPTER FIVE

Side dishes are as varied as cooks, and what appeals to one group may not appeal to another. The good thing about cooking with Dutch Ovens is whatever the taste of your guests in side dishes, they can be prepared in the black pot just as easily as in the home oven, whether it's corn on the cob, squash casserole, or asparagus fingers on a bed of wild rice.

The side dishes I picked for this book are some old favorites. One is a cowboy dish, another is a bean dish that is popular in the Northwoods, while another is a favorite with Boy and Girl Scouts as far back as their beginning.

What is your favorite side dish? You can make it in a Dutch Oven.

ANEEDA'S MACARONI & CHEESE

This is a recipe of my mom's that all who have ever eaten her cooking want. She was a school teacher in a remote country school when she met and married my dad, who was a trapper. She was always a great cook, and I think she inspired me later on to write and cook.

Portions: 4
Dutch Oven: 10-inch

INGREDIENTS

1 cup macaroni
1½ teaspoons salt
2 eggs
1 cup milk
Velveeta cheese, (about half a block)
1 cup breadcrumbs
pepper to taste
margarine for browning
pimento for topping

METHOD

1. Cook the macaroni in boiling water with ½ teaspoon salt until tender.

2. Beat the eggs, then add the milk and 1 teaspoon salt.

3. Add this mixture to the cooked macaroni.

4. Pour the macaroni into a 7-inch aluminum pan.

5. Put slices of Velveeta over the top of the macaroni.

6. Sprinkle the bread crumbs on top.

7. Place pats of margarine over the bread crumbs.

8. Sprinkle pimento or black pepper on top.

9. Bake until golden brown.

HIGH PLAINS HOMINY

This could be classified as a cowboy side dish, as I got the recipe many years ago from award–winning chuckwagon/Dutch Oven master chef Bill Cauble when he served it from the back of his chuckwagon while we were on a hunt. Bill, a native Texan, is the coauthor of Barbecue, Biscuits & Beans. *I have a lot of people who do not like hominy say they don't want to try the dish, but once they do, they usually come back for seconds.*

Portions: 5–6
Dutch Oven: 10-inch

INGREDIENTS

6 strips bacon
½ cup onion, chopped
2 cans yellow hominy
5 tablespoons salsa
1 cup cheddar cheese, grated
1 small can chilies, chopped
3 whole chilies

METHOD

1. Fry the bacon in a skillet and remove.

2. Sauté the onions in the bacon drippings until soft.

3. Place the onions, hominy, salsa, cheese, chopped chilies, and some of the bacon into a 9-inch aluminum pan. Mix to combine.

4. Put the pan on a trivet inside the Dutch Oven.

5. Arrange the whole chilies on top and then sprinkle on the remaining bacon.

6. Bake until the cheese is melted.

MISS PAM'S BEAN HOLE BEANS

My friends Ken and Pam French have a permanent bean hole at their cabin in Maine. Miss Pam is famous for her bean hole beans recipe. She uses aluminum foil to seal in the moisture of the dish, and I have found that the double aluminum foil seal does work some magic. Also, you will note that this dish cooks for a long time. Sometimes Ken puts it in the hot bean hole the night before they plan on serving the beans (See chapter 10 for details on bean hole cooking.)

Portions: 8
Dutch Oven: 12-inch

INGREDIENTS

2 pounds dry red kidney or Jacob
   Cattle beans
½ pound bacon, cut into pieces
¾ cup molasses
1¾ cups brown sugar
2 medium onions
2 teaspoons dry mustard
 salt and pepper

METHOD

1. Soak the beans in water for approximately 12 hours before putting them in a cast iron Dutch Oven.

2. Once they're done soaking, bring the beans to a boil.

3. Add the bacon, molasses, brown sugar, onions, mustard, salt, and pepper and stir well.

4. Cover and seal the top of the pot with aluminum foil. Leave enough slack so the top still fits on the pot snugly.

5. Place the lid on the foil, then cover tightly with aluminum foil again.

6. Bury in hot bean hole and cook approximately 15 hours.

JACK SQUASH

Squash was a favorite dish of Native Americans, and this cheesy squash side dish is always a hit.

Portions: 6–8
Dutch Oven: 12-inch

INGREDIENTS

3 pounds yellow squash
1 egg
2 large onions, chopped
2 tablespoons butter
20 soda crackers, crushed
2 cups pepper jack cheese, grated

METHOD

1. Boil squash with ½ teaspoon salt until soft then place in a colander to drain. Set aside to cool. Preheat the Dutch Oven.

2. Mash the squash and place in a greased 9-inch aluminum pan.

3. Whisk the egg and add it to the squash.

4. Sauté the onion in butter then add to the squash.

5. Add half the crushed crackers and 1½ cups of cheese and stir.

6. Sprinkle the remaining crackers and cheese on top.

7. Place in the preheated Dutch Oven on a cake rack.

8. Bake until the cheese melts and cracker crumbs turn golden brown.

STUFFED BAKED APPLES

This is an easy side dish that has been around for decades. It was a favorite back in my Boy Scout days. While it is usually served as a side dish, it is sometimes used as a dessert. It is a crowd pleaser and a great dish for the beginning Dutch Oven cook.

Portions: 4
Dutch Oven: 12-inch

INGREDIENTS

4 baking apples
⅓ cup raisins or dried cranberries
⅓ cup slivered almonds
½ teaspoon cinnamon
½ teaspoon nutmeg
2 cups water
4 ounces orange juice concentrate
2 tablespoons honey

METHOD

1. Wash the apples, then core them, leaving a little of the core on the bottom.

2. Combine the raisins, almonds, cinnamon, and nutmeg in a bowl, mixing well.

3. Stuff each apple with the mixture.

4. Combine the water, orange juice concentrate, and honey in a bowl. Mix well.

5. Place the stuffed apples in a 9-inch aluminum pan.

6. Pour the liquid mixture over the apples.

7. Place the pan on a trivet inside the Dutch Oven.

8. Bake until the apples are tender.

MISS BOBO'S SWEET POTATOES

I learned how to cook this dish at an Alabama Dutch Oven Gathering. I was told that this recipe came from Miss Bobo's Boarding House in Lynchburg, Tennessee. I have eaten at Miss Bobo's many times, and the food is always the best. Once you try this recipe, I'm sure you'll agree.

Portions: 6–8
Dutch Oven: 14-inch, Deep

INGREDIENTS

4 large sweet potatoes
¼ cup butter, softened
¾ cup sugar
⅛ teaspoon salt
¼ cup Jack Daniel's Tennessee
   Whiskey
½ cup pecan halves, lightly toasted

METHOD

1. Place the sweet potatoes in a large pan with just enough water to cover them.

2. Bring to a boil, cover, and cook until tender, about 35 minutes

3. Drain the water and let the potatoes cool, then peel off the skins.

4. In a mixing bowl, mash the potatoes with the butter.

5. Add the sugar, salt, and whiskey. Mix thoroughly.

6. Spread half of the potato mixture in a large, greased loaf pan. Sprinkle with half the pecans. Repeat.

7. Place the loaf pan in a Dutch Oven and bake until the mixture is hot throughout, approximately 30 minutes.

DESSERTS
CHAPTER SIX

When it comes to picking favorite dishes to be cooked in the Dutch Oven, I would be hard-pressed to find something I like better than desserts prepared in the black pots. It seems the pot adds something to a pie, cookies, cake, or cobblers that you just don't find in other ovens. These desserts seem a little more moist, tastier, and sweeter than the same dishes cooked by any other means.

The Dutch Oven is ideal for baking desserts.

When cooking desserts in your Dutch Oven, it would be wise to use an aluminum pizza pan or aluminum foil pan (see chapter 12), as sugar, fruit juices, and other sweets, if allowed to get on the cast iron, will be hard to remove and may require reseasoning the pot again.

Back in the days of old, cowboys, miners, explorers, and others spending long periods in the backcountry wrote of craving peaches and peach dishes. I have been where they were during my outdoor career so I know the value of peach cobblers and other sweet favorites, such as pineapple upside-down cake, apple pie, bread pudding, and coconut pie.

Here are some of my favorite ways of cooking them.

PINEAPPLE UPSIDE-DOWN CAKE

If your cooking gear includes a 10-inch pineapple upside-down cake pan, then this will be an easy dessert to cook. It is an ideal recipe to use when you have returned to camp after a full day afield.

Portions: 6
Dutch Oven: 12-inch

INGREDIENTS

¼ cup butter, softened
½ cup brown sugar
1 can pineapple slices, drained, reserve juice
1 small jar maraschino cherries
1 package Jiffy Golden Yellow Cake Mix
1 egg

METHOD

1. Preheat the Dutch Oven.

2. Melt the butter in the pineapple upside-down cake pan, then sprinkle the brown sugar on top.

3. Place pineapple slices in the pan, then place a cherry in the center of each slice. Set aside.

4. In a medium bowl, beat the yellow cake mix, egg, and half of the pineapple juice for 4 minutes.

5. Pour the batter into the pan over the pineapple slices. Place the pan on a trivet or cake rack inside the Dutch Oven.

6. Cook until the cake is golden brown and a toothpick inserted in the center comes out clean.

7. Remove the cake from the oven and pour the remaining pineapple juice over it. Allow the cake to cool in the pan for 2 minutes.

8. Carefully flip the cake onto a plate. Serve warm.

BUBBLY PEACH COBBLER

I was looking for a quick peach cobbler that tasted so good others would think a lot of time and skill went into its making. I discovered this jewel and it serves all of my wishes.

Portions: 6
Dutch Oven: 12-inch

INGREDIENTS

½ stick butter
4 cups peaches, peeled and sliced (can
   use canned)
1 cup sugar
1 cup flour
1 cup milk

METHOD

1. Preheat the Dutch Oven.

2. Melt the butter in the bottom of a 9-inch aluminum pan.

3. Add the peaches and sugar.

4. Stir in the flour and milk.

5. Place the cake pan on a trivet inside the Dutch Oven.

6. Bake until golden brown.

ROGER'S QUICK COBBLER

I'm one of the cooks on the chuckwagon crew known as the Flint River Chuck Wagon. The chief cook and owner of the chuckwagon is Roger Graves. We cook for many events where we are serving from twenty to seven hundred people in a short period of time. This recipe is a quick cobbler Roger came up with so we could serve a lot of people peach or blackberry cobbler quickly. He uses one-time-use aluminum foil cobbler pans so cleanup is easy.

Portions: 6
Dutch Oven: 12-inch

INGREDIENTS

½ stick butter
⅓ cup sugar
⅔ cup milk
1 package Louisiana Fish Fry Cobbler Mix
1½ can sliced peaches, save ½ can of juice (canned blackberries may be substituted)

METHOD

1. Preheat the Dutch Oven.

2. Melt the butter in an aluminum foil cobbler pan.

3. Combine the sugar, milk and cobbler mix in a bowl.

4. Pour into the cobbler pan and mix thoroughly with the melted butter.

5. Add in half a can of peach juice and the peaches, spreading them out evenly.

6. Carefully place the cobbler pan into the Dutch Oven and cook until the top is golden brown.

7. Serve hot.

FRENCH COCONUT PIE

Here is one of my all-time favorite Dutch Oven desserts. It is always a hit at patio cookouts.

Portions: 8
Dutch Oven: 12-inch

INGREDIENTS

1 egg
½ cup sugar
¼ cup butter, melted
1 teaspoon lemon juice
½ tsp vanilla
½ can angel flake coconut
1 8-inch pie crust

METHOD

1. Preheat the Dutch Oven.

2. Combine the egg, sugar, butter, lemon juice, vanilla, and coconut in a bowl, stirring until smooth.

3. Pour the mixture into the prepared pie crust.

4. Place the pie pan into a 9-inch aluminum pan, then place them inside the 12-inch Dutch Oven.

5. Bake until golden brown.

SOFEE'S APPLE PIE

Here is a family favorite. I think every Dutch Oven cook should have at least one apple pie recipe in his battery. It's not American to be without one.

Portions: 8
Dutch Oven: 12-inch

INGREDIENTS

6 cups Granny Smith apples, sliced
1 tablespoon lemon juice
½ cup sugar
½ teaspoon ground cinnamon
1 tablespoon butter
2 deep-dish pie crusts (thawed if using
   frozen crusts)

METHOD

1. Preheat the Dutch Oven.

2. Combine the apples, lemon juice, sugar, cinnamon, and butter in a large pot, then cook for 10 minutes.

3. Pour the cooked mixture into one of the pie shells set in a Pyrex pie dish or 9-inch aluminum pan.

4. Cut out strips to form latticework from the second crust. Then cut out apple, stem, and leaf shapes from the remaining dough (optional).

5. Create the latticework on top of the pie, then, if desired, add the apple, leaf, and stem cutouts on top.

6. Place the pie on a 9-inch cake rack inside the Dutch Oven.

7. Bake until golden brown.

CHUCKWAGON BREAD PUDDIN'

One of the best desserts you can serve from the back of a chuckwagon or from the outdoor dining table on your patio is bread pudding topped with a warm, sweet sauce. Here is a simple recipe I got from an old Canadian outfitter many years ago. A bourbon sauce that I got from Bill Cauble follows. Mighty tasty.

Portions: 6
Dutch Oven: 12-inch

INGREDIENTS

12 leftover biscuits or ½ loaf of Italian bread
2 eggs
1 (12-ounce) can evaporated milk
1 tablespoon butter
⅓ cup sugar
½ cup raisins
1 teaspoon ground nutmeg
1 tablespoon vanilla extract
1 tablespoon ground cinnamon

METHOD

1. Preheat the Dutch Oven.
2. Cut the bread into 1-inch cubes.
3. Whip the eggs in a bowl, then add the evaporated milk and combine.
4. Melt the butter and stir into the egg and milk mixture. Next, add the sugar, raisins, nutmeg, vanilla, and ½ tablespoon of cinnamon.
5. Place the bread into a 9-inch aluminum pan.
6. Pour the mixture over the bread and mix until the bread is soggy.
7. Sprinkle the remaining cinnamon over the top.
8. Place the pan into the Dutch Oven and bake until it's brown.
9. Serve hot with the Bourbon Sauce on top.

BOURBON SAUCE

INGREDIENTS

½ cup butter, melted
½ cup sugar
½ cup half-and-half
1 tablespoon vanilla
½ cup bourbon, rum or amaretto, your taste

METHOD

1. Mix all ingredients in a cast iron pan and bring to a low boil.
2. Pour over the bread pudding while it's hot.

TRIPLE CHOCOLATE DELIGHT

If you have chocolate lovers in your family or at camp, then this will be a late-night favorite around the fire ring. It is quick and easy to bake.

Portions: 8–10
Dutch Oven: 12-inch

INGREDIENTS

1 chocolate cake mix (add eggs and oil if called for in the directions)
1 (24-ounce) package chocolate chips
1 can chocolate frosting

METHOD

1. Mix the cake as per the instructions on the box.

2. Add the chocolate chips to the cake batter and mix to combine.

3. Line the Dutch Oven with aluminum foil and spray the foil with cooking spray.

4. Pour the cake batter into the Dutch Oven and bake until a toothpick inserted in the center comes out clean.

5. Allow the cake to cool before frosting it.

6. Serve with ice cream.

CHAPTER SEVEN

One thing I have learned in a lifetime of Dutch Oven cooking: there are no experts. Some cooks are beginners, some are average, and some are above average, but all in one form or another are students. I think that is one of the things most of us like about this wonderful method of cooking: it is education and experience in progress.

This chapter is not a crash course that will make you an instant master of Dutch Oven cooking. However, it does provide tips that build on the foundation you will have after reading this book. These tips will take you to the next level of cooking and will make the actual experience of cooking in a Dutch Oven more successful and fun.

FOLLOW RECIPES EXACTLY

By taking shortcuts that didn't work, I have learned that the cook should follow recipes exactly, at least the first time. Good recipes result in good food when they are followed to the letter. After you have tried it successfully then you can put your own spin on it.

One word of caution: I have found a lot of poorly thought-out recipes that were supposed to be designed for Dutch Oven cooking. Be cautious when trying a new recipe from an unproven source. It may be bad from the start. This can cause a new cook to lose confidence. And don't try out an unproven recipe on the boss to show off your Dutch Oven cooking skills.

There is one exception to following recipes exactly—recipes that contain cooking times can get you in trouble fast. Don't trust published cooking times. The wind, air temperature, humidity, type and amount of coals, and many more factors will make cooking times for the same dish vary, sometimes greatly. A recipe cooked in Minnesota on a 28-degree day with

Be sure to carefully read and follow recipes to the letter. There are many good recipe books written for Dutch Oven cooking.

Dutch Ovens hold in more liquids than conventional cooking pots so adjust liquids accordingly.

a 10-mile-an-hour north wind blowing will be far different in cooking time than the same recipe cooked in the sun in Georgia on a 90-degree day with 98 percent humidity.

Use your own judgement and experience for cooking times. I have seen cooking times for the same dish vary by one hour under different conditions.

Follow good recipes to the letter, and collect good recipes like they were gold pieces.

LEARN TO ADJUST LIQUIDS

The Dutch Oven has a lid on it that fits tight when cooking and lets little moisture escape. That is great for some dishes and not so great for others. Recipes out of regular cookbooks usually don't take that into account. They are written for standard cookware that lets a good bit of moisture escape. Because of this, any liquids used in cooking, such as water, milk, juices, etc., may make the finished dish too moist. Make notes and adjust the amount of liquid next time.

IF CALLED FOR, PREHEAT THE POT AND LID

When a recipe calls for a preheated oven, take the time to preheat both the pot and lid. Be careful not to overdo it, as you could damage the vessel. I have found that many recipes designed specifically for Dutch Ovens start with a cool oven, but some, and many regular cookbook recipes, call for a preheated oven.

Also, I have learned that many new cooks burn their bread and pies on the bottom while the top is only half done. By heating the Dutch Oven lid before it is placed on the pot the heat can be balanced. As more experience is gained, the proper mix of coals from top to bottom will straighten out this bottom-burning problem.

Aluminum pizza pans can go a long way toward protecting a Dutch Oven from acidic foods. They are available in many sizes.

CONSIDER USING A CAKE RACK AND PAN WHEN PRACTICAL

When I started using a cake rack and heavy-duty aluminum cake pans when making certain dishes in a Dutch Oven, it made my cooking go much smoother, and oven cleanup is a snap. Almost anything that can be baked can be baked this way. I use them for cooking beans, bread, chili, and dishes that contain a lot of sugar that I think might cause me to have to reseason my Dutch Ovens. They do hold less food than an empty oven, and you may have to take a recipe to the next size Dutch Oven or refigure the amounts of the recipe ingredients. However, it is a small price to pay for the positive results.

MATCH RECIPE TO DUTCH OVEN SIZE

One of the most common problems some beginning Dutch Oven cooks have is choosing the size oven needed for a recipe. Most recipes designed for Dutch Ovens will have the required oven size indicated. However, most of the recipes we use are for kitchen pots of various sizes and must be converted to match a Dutch Oven size. Cooking a 2-quart banana pudding in which the recipe calls for a 10-inch oven in a 14-inch oven will quickly result in burned pudding, as it barely covers the bottom of the 8-quart pot. (See chapter 1 for average Dutch Oven capacities.) Take the time to study new recipes and match them with the capacity of your ovens and the pans used in the ovens. Keep notes. You will be glad you did.

A heavy-duty pot lifter is necessary for lifting aluminum pans of food from a hot Dutch Oven.

Stay focused when cooking. A few moments of distraction can spoil a meal. It is a good time to relax.

HAVE ENOUGH CHARCOAL OR WOOD ON HAND

There is nothing more frustrating than being halfway through a cooking session and running out of fuel or not having hot coals ready to replace burned down coals. Keep a good supply of charcoal or seasoned hardwood on hand for the meals you have planned. Cold temperatures, wind, overcast, shade, or high humidity can cause a cooking session to use more fuel than expected, so be ready for the unexpected. You don't want to run out of charcoal halfway through cooking Thanksgiving dinner.

Also, think ahead. Plan to have enough hot coals to cook your entire meal at constant temperatures. Suddenly realizing your briquettes are about burned out is not the time to start heating up replacements. Your Dutch Ovens will start to cool while you heat new coals and the meal outcome will be less than desired. Keep hot campfire coals and briquettes ready for when you may need them. When cooking for groups, I like to have a helper whose job it is to make sure I have plenty of hot coals throughout the cooking process.

STAY WITH THE OVEN(S)

I hear from a lot of Dutch Oven chefs who complain about burning food after learning the basics of temperature control or who say cooking time takes longer than expected. During the conversation, you find out that they do not stay with their ovens during cooking or they are so busy talking that they do not watch their pots. Successful Dutch Oven chefs enjoy watching their pots and keeping the temperature steady. They rotate their pots and lids regularly. They do not let their coals burn too low or burn too hot. Good Dutch Oven cooking requires some attention to the cooking process. To me, this is relaxing time, with my mind on little else but the cooking process.

DON'T SNEAK A PEEK TOO OFTEN

If you want to upset master chef George Prechter, just let him see you lift the lid of his Dutch Ovens frequently to check the dish. One of the wonderful features of a Dutch Oven is that the heavy lid seals in moisture. Every time you lift the lid, moisture escapes and the inside temperature decreases. When you are learning how to cook in a Dutch Oven, it is necessary to peek every five to ten

Resist the temptation to look in the pot every few minutes.

minutes just to learn temperature control, etc., but once you get the hang of it, resist the temptation. Prechter suggest that "dish checks" should not occur more often than every fifteen minutes and the peek should not last longer than two to three seconds unless stirring is necessary. Many seasoned cooks rarely, if ever, lift the lid on their ovens. That know-how and confidence comes with experience.

BLACK FOOD OR METALLIC TASTE

If the food you are cooking in your Dutch Ovens turns black or gets a metallic taste, this tells you that several things are wrong: either your oven is improperly seasoned, the quality of seasoning is poor, or the food is left in the pot for too long after cooking. Remember, cast iron vessels are not food-storage vessels, even for short periods of time. It is best to remove food from your oven as soon as it is cooked and place it in a serving dish. Always clean your oven as soon as possible with boiling water and brush. Rinse and dry thoroughly. Wipe inside and out with a light coat of Crisco. (While the black food that comes from an oven that needs reseasoning is not pleasant to look at, it will not hurt you.) If the problem persists, reseason the oven and lid.

DEALING WITH ACIDIC FOODS

Acidic foods, such as tomatoes and beans, are hard on the seasoning of a Dutch Oven and will often require you to reseason your oven. It has been my experience that anytime I cook beans of any type in my cast iron ovens, they need to be reseasoned. At first I tried cleaning out the pot immediately after the beans were done, but most of the time the pot still needed reseasoning. For this reason, I like to cook beans and any highly acid foods in heavy-duty aluminum cake pans in the Dutch Oven on most occasions. Other than spillover, this protects my ovens and makes cleanup easy. When I do cook highly acid dishes—such as stews, spaghetti sauce, soups, or chili—without cake pans in my ovens, I try to use parchment paper liners.

As soon as food is done, remove it from the hot oven or you can expect overcooked or soggy food.

DUTCH OVENS COOL SLOWLY

One of the things we like most about cast iron Dutch Ovens can come back to bite you in the rear if you don't watch it. We like the ovens because they hold heat very well. However, when you cook a dish and remove the oven from the coals, it keeps on cooking for a while. This can ruin some dishes. I once cooked a beef tenderloin for a group in my 16-inch oven. They were emphatic that they wanted it cooked medium rare. And it was—when I removed the oven from the coals. But I got busy with other cooking chores and forgot to remove the tenderloin. When I did remove it, it was well done. The beautiful piece of choice meat kept cooking in the hot oven.

Any dishes you do not want to keep cooking should be removed from the oven when it is removed from the coals.

USE SEVERAL OVENS AT ONCE

During my early years of Dutch Oven cooking, I had only one 10-inch oven. It took forever to cook bread, main dish, and a pie. When I got to one dish, the other was cold. Then I discovered the value of having several Dutch Ovens where I could cook an entire meal at the same time. Using stack cooking, I could cook a meal in the same space I once cooked with a single oven.

Invest in several ovens and enjoy the pleasure of cooking an entire meal in a short period of time. Also, as more family and friends discover your cooking talent, you will have more dinner guests to feed.

TAG YOUR POTS AND LIDS

If you have several Dutch Ovens the same size or go to Dutch Oven events where you are cooking with other Dutch Oven owners you will want to place a metal tag on each pot and matching lid. It is easy to get lids and pots mixed up, and then finding the matching lid for a pot can be difficult. Chuckwagon Supply offers metal tags with rings that can fit on your Dutch Oven lid loop and on the pot side where the bail is attached. They come with your initials and pot/lid number. A set of these tags on your ovens keeps someone from accidentally taking home your oven or your matching lid getting permanently separated from its pot.

ATTEND DUTCH OVEN GATHERINGS AND COOK-OFFS

One of the best places to learn new cooking techniques, proven new recipes, and meet fellow Dutch Oven cooks is at one of the many, and growing in number, Dutch Oven gatherings and cook-offs held throughout the country. Also, Dutch Oven cooking is a major part of chuckwagon and many wild game cook-offs. A day spent talking to, and observing, the cooks who enjoy this activity can give you a wealth of information on the subject. I learned more about what I was doing wrong and the best ways to do it right in one Saturday morning at a Dutch Oven cook-off than I would have in a year on my own. And I can say firsthand, you will meet some of the best people to call new friends. If you are serious about Dutch Oven cooking, this will be one of your best investments of time.

To learn the location and dates of cook-offs, go to the websites of the Dutch Oven societies listed in the appendix of this book.

JOIN IDOS

The International Dutch Oven Society (IDOS) is an organization you should be a member of if you are reading this book. This organization is the clearinghouse for the dissemination of information, education, and fellowship when it comes to Dutch Oven cooking. Their quarterly newsletter, The IDOS Dutch Oven News, covers a wide range of interesting subjects. One issue may include information on judging a cook-off, new product information, tips on cooking with a little 5-inch oven, recipes, how to build a Dutch Oven cooking table, member news, and cooking tips. The newsletter alone is well worth the membership fee. To learn more about this organization, go to their website. There you will also find a wealth of Dutch Oven recipes and other worthwhile information.

LEARN FROM YOUR MISTAKES AND HAVE FUN

There aren't many foods I know of that can't be cooked in a Dutch Oven and taste better for the effort. Anyone can master the skill with a little effort, as Dutch Oven cooking is easy once you know the basics. It is an ongoing learning process that is most enjoyable. Don't let learning the basics discourage you. Learn from your mistakes and expand your skills with new and exciting recipes. Most importantly, have fun as you enjoy some of the best tasting food in the world.

CHAPTER EIGHT

My first few years of cooking meals in cast iron Dutch Ovens were done in wilderness settings using coals from campfires as a heat source. Then I discovered the fun of cooking for family and friends in the backyard. In this setting, it was not possible to have a campfire going from which to get shovels of hot coals to heat my ovens. It was this backyard cooking that introduced me to charcoal briquettes to heat my ovens, and I have been hooked ever since.

Charcoal briquettes are the easiest way to cook in Dutch Ovens. They give a longer, more steady supply of heat, which aids greatly in controlling temperature.

At this point, I should point out that a lot of Dutch Oven chefs like to use lump charcoal; however, I have found the briquettes to work much better. Lump charcoal does not burn as uniformly as briquettes so it is harder to control cooking temperatures. Lump charcoal burns hotter and does not last as long as briquettes. So given a choice between lump charcoal or charcoal briquettes I choose briquettes.

Charcoal briquettes have campfire coals beat in several ways. First, they do not require the work, time, and fuel involved with building a campfire. Using a charcoal chimney starter, charcoal briquettes do not take but a few minutes to be ready to place on and under the oven. Quality charcoal briquettes burn longer and more evenly than campfire coals. Briquettes are easier to place around Dutch Ovens, and to move around, than loose coals. Under ideal conditions, quality briquettes burn for approximately one hour, campfire coals about half that. Briquettes are easy to transport and much easier to clean up than campfire ashes.

ARRANGING BRIQUETTES FOR CONTROLLED HEATING

Arranging charcoal for temperature control is a personal thing with Dutch Oven chefs and the subject of many campfire and backyard debates. Some like to lay

Cast iron is well-known for holding heat evenly for long periods and the proper placement of charcoal briquettes helps the cook get the most effective baking from his Dutch Oven.

their briquettes in a checkerboard pattern, both under the oven and on the lid. Others like to place their briquettes in a circle under and on top of the oven. And yet others like to use a circle of briquettes under the oven and a checkerboard on the lid. I have eaten some great dishes cooked by chefs who used each of the three methods so it depends on which method you choose to master. Personally, I like the circle arrangement.

One charcoal briquette pattern that almost all Dutch Oven cooks agree on is the pattern used for frying or boiling. Since a lot of heat is required for these two methods of cooking, a full spread of briquettes is used under the oven. As the oil or water heats up, the heat can be reduced by removing a few briquettes using tongs.

For most dishes cooked in a Dutch Oven, one of five temperatures are called for: 325 degrees, 350 degrees, 375 degrees, 400 degrees, or 425 degrees. (I have found that majority of my dishes are cooked at 350 degrees and other Dutch Oven cooks tell me they usually cook at 350 degrees.) Obtaining and maintaining these temperatures is a challenge for the Dutch Oven cook, as wind, air temperature, sun, shade, humidity, ashes, and brand of charcoal can influence the cooking temperature. A strong wind can make the briquettes burn extremely hot; accumulation of ashes on the briquettes can make them burn cool. Cold outside air can make the pot colder than usual, and high temperatures can increase the cooking temperature. A high humidity can make briquettes burn slow, thus less heat. Whether the cooking is done in the sun or shade can make a difference—some cooks say it can make a 25-degree difference in cooking temperature. The point is, you must make adjustments in the number of briquettes used depending on these local conditions. For all these reasons, I never give cooking times for any of my recipes.

Having said that, I will give some commonly accepted guidelines for the arrangement and number of charcoal briquettes to use for Dutch Oven cooking. I have used these guidelines with satisfaction and they are the guidelines suggested by Lodge Manufacturing Company for use with their Dutch Ovens. I strongly suggest you keep a notebook handy when you are cooking under different weather conditions and keep records as to the briquette arrangement and the number of briquettes you use for reaching the desired cooking temperatures under the conditions. That is some of the fun and rewards of being a master of Dutch Oven cooking.

ESTIMATING TEMPERATURE

The following baking temperature chart will get you started, and with a little experience you will be making a few changes for your local conditions. The bold number to the right of the oven sizes is the total number of briquettes required to reach the temperature. The numbers directly below those are the number of top/bottom briquettes required to attain the temperature.

BAKING TEMPERATURE CHART (approximate)

Oven Size	Temperature Desired (*F*)				
	325	350	375	400	425
8-inch	**15**	**16**	**17**	**18**	**19**
	10/5	11/5	11/6	12/6	13/6
10-inch	**19**	**21**	**23**	**25**	**28**
	13/6	14/7	16/7	17/8	19/9
12-inch	**23**	**25**	**27**	**29**	**31**
	16/7	17/8	18/9	19/10	21/10
14-inch	**30**	**32**	**34**	**36**	**38**
	20/10	21/11	22/12	24/12	25/13
16-inch	**34**	**36**	**37**	**40**	**42**
	22/12	24/12	24/13	27/13	28/14

Courtesy of Lodge Manufacturing Company.

Using long-handled tongs, arrange the number of briquettes needed by placing them under the oven's bottom in a circular pattern so that they are a half-inch inside the oven's edge. Arrange the briquettes on top of the lid in a circle around the edge with one on either side of the handle.

Avoid the temptation to pile all the coals in one bunch, either under the oven or on the lid. When this is done, a hot spot forms, guaranteeing burned food and possibly ruining the oven.

Dutch Oven chef George Prechter recommends picking up the oven off the coals every 15 minutes and rotating it a quarter turn. Then lift the lid and rotate it a quarter turn in the opposite direction. This helps prevent hot spots from forming.

All of this sounds difficult to learn, but it is quite easy and a fun process, especially the testing. I used biscuits as a test food when I was working out the number of briquettes and configuration to use on a new 10-inch Dutch Oven. I kept a jar of homemade muscadine jam nearby and used it on the test biscuits I didn't burn. Soon I had all my neighbors helping with the test.

I have some friends who don't depend on experience to judge the temperature inside their Dutch Ovens. They use a long-stemmed oven thermometer. Anytime they want to know the temperature inside the oven, they ease the lid of their oven open and insert the thermometer inside and read the temperature. Many do this too often. It allows moisture and heat to escape and increases the chance of ashes getting into the food. There is also a greater chance of getting burned when doing this. You be the judge.

A growing number of cooks now use an infrared laser thermometer to measure the exterior pot temperature. It is accurate and keeps the cook a distance from the fire and it does not require opening the pot.

Like any new cooking technique, practice is required to master Dutch Oven temperature control, but once you have a system that works, Dutch Oven cooking is easy.

CHARCOAL SAFETY

Keep these safety tips in mind as you use charcoal for your Dutch Oven cooking:

1. Never burn charcoal inside homes, buildings, tents, vehicles, etc., as odorless toxic fumes may accumulate and cause death.
2. Never use gasoline to light charcoal.

3. Do not add lighter fuel directly to burning or hot charcoal.
4. After cooking, make sure ashes are completely cool before discarding.
5. Cook safely away from flammable items, overhanging roofs or limbs, and out of the way of playing children or sports activities.

COOKING WITH CAMPFIRE COALS
CHAPTER NINE

Successfully cooking a Dutch Oven meal with coals from a campfire requires more experience than cooking with charcoal briquettes.

It requires learning how to judge the amount of coals to place on and under the oven, heat output from the coals, what coals burn best, and when to replace coals.

When I first started Dutch Oven cooking, I thought the more hot coals from the campfire, the better, and I burned a lot of food. My scoutmaster said I cremated everything I placed in a Dutch Oven. Also, it took me a couple of ruined meals to learn that wood like pine, poplar, and cottonwood didn't make good coals for Dutch Oven cooking. However, it didn't take me too long to "get the feel" of campfire cooking, and it's been easy ever since.

DESIGN A CAMPFIRE FOR COOKING

The location of your cooking site will have a lot to do with the type of fire you build to heat coals for your Dutch Oven cooking. Obviously in many areas you cannot use an open fire and charcoal briquettes will be your only choice. However, you may live in an area where you can have an open fire in your backyard and you may install a commercial or homemade fire ring, or you may be in a backcountry camp where you can put in a key hole fire with rocks for days of cooking, or you may be on the move where a simple fire ring will have to do. The point is, there is a campfire design for all situations that will give you a good supply of coals for your Dutch Ovens.

COMMERCIAL FIRE RINGS

It's hard to beat an oak or hickory bed of coals.

For those lucky enough to live where it is permissible to have an open fire in their backyard, the commercial fire ring is a safe way to have a fire that produces hot coals for Dutch Oven cooking. I have visited many ranches in the West where Dutch Oven suppers were the norm, cooked on the patio using an open fire. Many of these ranches have put in an all-steel commercial fire ring. A lot of state and national parks have commercial fire rings that work well for Dutch Oven cooking while camping. I had a commercial fire ring at my cabin in Cross Creek Hollow, and it was the favorite gathering place for visitors, especially if the Dutch Ovens were heating. It had a heavy-duty grill that could be lowered on the fire for frying or boiling in a Dutch Oven, and when the grill was not needed, it was swung back out of the way to make shoveling hot coals easy.

When I was looking for my fire ring, I found it difficult to find a commercial source for them, and I was lucky to have a friend who had an extra one. Since then, I have found several sources. A manufacturer with a good variety of fire rings is Pilot Rock Park Equipment Company. They have fire rings with adjustable cooking grates. The grate tips back out of the way so as not to interfere with getting coals for Dutch Ovens or obstruct the view of people sitting around the campfire during storytelling sessions. Here are some other features of these well-made fire rings:

- Flanged fire ring. The 1-inch top flange is both a safety feature and reinforces the ring against heat warpage.
- Infinite adjustment of cooking surface. You can adjust the grate for various cooking levels.
- Grate tips back for easy fire building. Grate will lift up and out of the ring for fire building and cleaning out.
- Three fire barrier heights. Rings are available with 7-inch, 9-inch, or 11¼-inch height. Choose the degree of fire barrier you need.
- Unique handle design. The handle design allows the cooking grate to lower down inside the ring and keeps the spring grips out of the heat.
- Public-use-type spring grips. The spring grips are coiled from ½-inch steel flat bar for a safer, cooler handle.
- Fire ring tips back for easy cleaning. The entire ring lifts up on hinges to make cleaning easy.
- Installs without a concrete pad. The fire ring may be installed on the ground or on gravel, avoiding the trouble and expense of a concrete pad.
- Conserves firewood. The cooking grate will lower down inside ring, allowing the user to cook over a low fire.

The keyhole fire ring is ideal for the camp kitchen, especially when Dutch Ovens are used.

- Reinforced grate foils vandalism. The structurally reinforced grate design is strong enough to deter vandalism.

Pilot Rock makes fire rings in a variety of diameters, ranging from a wood-conserving 28 inches to a group size of 60 inches. They also make models that are wheelchair accessible and models that are raised high enough for cooking comfort.

If you don't need all the advantages of a commercial fire ring, you can make one from a large truck or tractor tire rim by taking a cutting torch and cutting out the middle. However, since the fire ring is an item you will probably buy only once for your use, why not get the commercial model with all the conveniences?

THE KEYHOLE FIRE

Many years ago when I first started going into the backcountry of the Rocky Mountains, I noticed that several of the old outfitters who cooked in Dutch Ovens used a campfire design they called a keyhole fire. They would pick a safe and logical location for the cooking fire and would take rocks and make an outline that was shaped like a keyhole, round at one end and a rectangle running from it. The round part would be up to 36 inches in diameter, and the rectangle part would be from 12 to 24 inches wide and about 36 inches long. A fire of choice hardwood would be built in the round part and then hot coals would be pulled out into the rectangle part. Here it would be easy to get a shovel of coals to put on Dutch Ovens without disturbing the main fire. Also, the narrow part of the keyhole would be used to place a grill to sit Dutch Ovens on for stewing or frying. It was a most efficient arrangement for long-term base camp cooking.

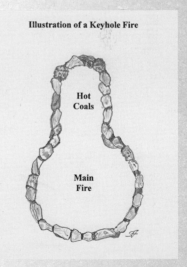

Illustration of a Keyhole Fire

Hot Coals

Main Fire

Keyhole fire ring

Cooking with hardwood fueling the Dutch Oven dates back to the earliest days of the oven. It still works well today.

COOKING PLATFORM

Regardless of what type of campfire you choose to use, you will need a flat, level surface upon which to place your hot coals and Dutch Ovens. Cold, wet ground will rob the ovens of heat rapidly and leave scorched earth. Many Dutch Oven cooks have a heavy-duty, flat piece of metal they use as a cooking platform. Others carry a folding steel cooking table, such as is used with charcoal briquette cooking, for use with campfire coals. I have seen many backcountry cooks place a large flat rock near the campfire for this purpose. I use a flat rock adjacent to the fire ring at my cabin. And, when commercial fire rings are permanently placed, a concrete pad is often poured, specifically to create a safe, level location for Dutch Oven cooking.

No matter what type of fire ring you use with an open fire, you will need a safe, level place in which to cook in Dutch Ovens. So take some time to scout out a good spot for your ovens. I once spilled a stew in front of a lot of people because I hastily picked a cooking spot near my campfire. The ground gave way under the weight of the full cast iron oven, and my guests watched their dinner run out on the ground. That was many years ago, but I still hear about it today.

CHOICE OF COOKING WOOD

One of the fun debates you will often hear when a group of Dutch Oven cooks get together, especially if they are from different parts of the United States, is what type of firewood burns into the best coals to use for Dutch Oven cooking. Chuckwagon cooks from the southwest will fight for mesquite, southern cooks will argue for hickory, northern cooks will brag about oak, and some midwestern cooks swear by Osage orange.

Several years ago, I received a call from a new Dutch Oven cook from Louisiana. This cook was having trouble getting his dishes done, through and through, before the outer edges of the food were burned. It was obvious that at some point his oven was getting too hot, but it was strange that the food was still raw in the center. At some point, I asked him about the wood he was burning for his coals. It was pine. That answered all the questions. The pine was burning hot for a short period of time but burned out quickly. Softwoods are not for Dutch Oven cooking, except possibly for kindling to get a hardwood fire going.

What the Dutch Oven cook wants is a heat-holding coal that will burn evenly and hot for long periods of time. Consider only proven hardwood fuel wood for making coals for Dutch Oven cooking.

Unfortunately not all hardwoods produce good coals for Dutch Oven cooking. Poor choices of hardwoods are poplar, cherry, elm, aspen, birch, gum, cottonwood, and sycamore, to name a few. They will make a good conversation fire, and kindling for starting fires, but will not give hot, long-lasting coals for cooking in Dutch Ovens.

Give the highest consideration to hickory, oak, mesquite, and hard maple, in my opinion, in that order. I have friends who are master chefs with the Dutch Oven who prefer other woods. Medrick Northrop, a great cook in the bush or at home, spent much of his outdoor career in Alaska. His wood of choice for Dutch Oven cooking is pecan—something that is in short supply where he lives. The late Ken French, known as the "woods wizard" in his home state of Maine, liked walnut. I once watched him make coals for Dutch Oven cooking using a supply of "factory reject" rifle stocks. That was some of the most beautiful wood I have ever seen go into a campfire.

Other Dutch Oven cooks agree with me about hickory. Arizona Dutch Oven expert Stella Hughes writing in her well-known book, *Bacon & Beans*, states: "I've only had one experience in using hickory wood and it made me a lifetime disciple of this wonderful hardwood. Hickory burns down to a bed of hot coals that keeps an even, generous heat for hours."

Supply can have a lot to do with the wood you choose for your Dutch Oven campfire, but given a choice, use hickory, oak, mesquite, or hard maple and you will have some good coals for your ovens.

OBTAINING AND STORING HARDWOOD FIREWOOD

If you do a lot of cooking using campfire coals, you will want a supply of firewood.

If you plan on buying firewood, then the density of a wood is important since wood is usually bought by volume. The most common unit is the cord—a stack of wood 4 feet wide, 4 feet high,

A good supply of hardwood seasoning in a woodshed can give the Dutch Oven cook many pleasant meals. Invite those you cook for over to help when it's time to put up the wood.

and 8 feet long. Sometimes wood is sold by the truckload, which is a highly variable measure. A rule of thumb is that a half-ton pickup truck is capable of carrying one-third cord of wood. To find out what fraction of a cord you are buying, use this formula: height of wood multiplied by width of wood multiplied by depth of wood divided by 128. The answer is the fraction of a cord.

The tighter the wood is packed, the more wood for your money. The denser the wood, the fewer trips you will have to make to the woodshed.

With a little effort on your part and a one-time investment in tools, including chain saw, wedges, bow saw, ax, files, hearing protection, safety glasses, and maul, you can get wood for free or for little cost. If your home or cabin is sitting on wooded acreage, a rule of thumb is that with proper management, one cord of wood can be cut annually for each acre you own. (A local forest ranger or forester can advise you as to how to manage this forest.) This practice will keep your wood supply renewable as well as beautify your woodlands by removing old and diseased trees.

The U.S.D.A. Forest Service and some state forests have programs to permit the public to cut firewood of down or dead trees for little or no cost. Other free or low-cost sources of wood are utility company pruning, pulp and paper companies, sawmills, town dumps, and farmers clearing new ground. Always be sure to secure permission from the proper authorities.

As a side note, I always watch for new house construction when driving around. This is sometimes a good free source of hardwood flooring scraps, which can be split into Dutch Oven fuel. Most builders will be glad for you to haul it away.

If you don't want to cut your own wood, you can usually find a local firewood dealer. When buying wood, be sure it is split and dry (why pay for water?), dense, and tightly packed. If you must buy green wood, buy it in the early spring since it takes months to dry. Be sure to measure your fire ring and have your firewood cut small enough to fit.

Once you have the wood, how do you prepare it for burning? If it is moist, it should be air-dried before use. If the wood's diameter is greater than 8 inches, it should be split and the length cut small enough to fit your fire ring and to stack easily in the woodshed. Split wood dries faster than wood that is not split and is easier to stack. Stacking firewood off the ground will permit air to circulate freely in the woodshed and will help prevent ground rot.

Stacking the wood in a sunny location and covering it with clear plastic sheeting can accelerate the drying of wood. It is best to keep the plastic away from the ends of the woodpile to allow good airflow, which speeds the evaporation process.

An interesting and fast method for drying firewood is the use of a solar wood dryer. This easy-to-build device is simply a rack for stacking cut firewood off the ground. The rack is placed in a sunny spot near the cabin and loaded with hardwood. Next, the wood and rack are wrapped in clear plastic except the ends. A vent opening is designed into the top of the dryer. The sun and air speed up the drying process. This is a good method to dry wood if you are cutting your firewood late in the season.

One way to tell if wood is ready for burning is to weigh a few identified pieces on a bathroom scale. Record the weight and place the identified wood back into the woodpile. Wait a month and then weigh the wood again. If the wood has lost weight, it is drying.

Another method for determining if wood is ready for burning is to examine the ends of the logs to see if cracks are appearing. Cracks appear only when wood is relatively dry.

Store your supply of firewood in a woodshed to keep it dry and from getting scattered. My woodshed is small, but it holds enough wood to keep me in cooking fuel for months. It is made from treated lumber and measures 8 feet wide by 4 feet deep by 6 ½ inches tall in the front. In the front of the shed is a large wooden box that holds split kindling. My sons and I built the shed in one day, so a woodshed is not a major project.

START THE FIRE EARLY

Good hardwood burns slow, so be sure to start your fire early before you need to start cooking. I once saw a young, inexperienced chuckwagon cook, preparing his first supper on the trail, build a mesquite fire less than ten minutes before the hungry cowboys came in to eat. The meal wasn't ready until two hours after they arrived. That young man learned a very valuable lesson that night and was reminded of it for years.

Keep a long-handled shovel near your hardwood fire for transporting coals.

Start your hardwood fire at least forty-five minutes before you need hot coals.

TOOLS FOR CAMPFIRE COOKING

Besides the tools normally needed for Dutch Oven cooking, you will also need a long-handled shovel for moving coals from the fire to your ovens. As I stated earlier in this book, many cooks drill holes in their shovel to allow ashes and smaller than desired coals to fall out.

A whisk broom is handy when using campfire coals as you are always dealing with fine ashes and the broom is a good way to keep the oven lid clean when removing it.

Keeping firewood cut in a size to fit your fire ring calls for a sharp hatchet and the knowledge of how to use it properly and safely. Remember, it doesn't take a large fire to produce good coals, so keep the fire small with small pieces of wood.

A long handle poker is a must to keep the burning firewood under control.

JUDGING COOKING TIME

When cooking with coals from an open campfire, it can be difficult to judge cooking times until you have gotten a lot of experience. No book, not even this one, is going to be able to provide cooking guidelines so that your food will never burn. Like charcoal briquettes, when using campfire coals, heating values are determined, in part, by humidity, wind, shade, temperature, etc. Another factor, unlike charcoal briquettes, is the type of wood burning and the amount of coals placed on and under the oven—the latter varies greatly from person to person. It is much easier to tell someone how many charcoal briquettes to use than

Use a whisk broom to remove ashes from the lid for refueling or when you're ready to remove your food from the Dutch Oven.

Resist the temptation to heap coals on the oven or sit it in the fire. That will guarantee burned food.

it is how many shovelfuls of coals, of an undetermined size, to use.

Here are some tips to follow as you get experience.

1. When taking coals from the fire to the ovens, try to get coals of about the same size. Here is where a shovel with holes in it is valuable.

2. Resist the temptation to heap hot coals under and over the oven. It takes fewer coals than most people think. You simply need the oven to be hot, not an inferno.

3. Place coals in a 2:1 ratio, top to bottom. If you place a quarter shovelful of coals under a 10-inch oven, place a half shovelful on the lid.

4. Keep the coals under the bottom in a circle toward the outside of the pot. The coals on the lid should be placed around the inside of the flange. Coals heaped under or on an oven can cause hot spots and unevenly cooked food.

5. Resist the temptation to bury the oven in the campfire. I know that sounds unnecessary to say, but there are people who do it and wonder why their food is burned beyond recognition. There is a lot of magic in the black pots but not that much.

6. Always, when cooking with campfire coals, turn the oven a quarter turn every 15 minutes and the lid a quarter turn in the opposite direction. This prevents hot spots and helps keep the cooking temperature even.

7. While learning to judge cooking temperature, open the pot every 15 minutes and check the doneness of the food. Keep notes, including the type and amount of wood used. Eventually you will get a feel for cooking time and will be the envy of those who watch you work your magic.

8. Be sure to keep an eye on the coals under and over the oven. Coals from a campfire do not burn as long as charcoal briquettes and must be replenished regularly.

9. Stay with your cooking; many a meal has been ruined by a cook forgetting he was on duty.

Create a solid, level cooking platform near the fire; this is where you will cook with the Dutch Oven.

By keeping careful notes and remembering the details of your cooking sessions, it will not take you long to "get the feel" for cooking with campfire coals. This is one of the times it is okay to take a peek at the food as it cooks. These inspections will teach you when to add coals and when to brush a few away.

SAFETY TIPS

Anytime you are cooking around an open fire, you must keep the actions and safety of others in mind. Keep children and adults that act like children away from the fire and hot ovens.

During a hunting trip I was cooking with an experienced Dutch Oven team for a group of wounded heroes. When the meal was complete and we were cleaning up, Johnny Ikard, a master campfire chef, took the lid off a hot oven with a lid lifter and set it next to the cool ovens. I came along and quickly, thinking it was cool, picked up the hot lid with my bare hand. I left my fingerprints on that lid loop. Always consider cast iron hot until proven otherwise.

Use fire safety and common sense when working with fire. Many grass, brush, and forest fires have been started by campfires.

Keep hatchets and other sharp tools in a safe place and out of reach of curious hands.

Keep an eye on the wind, and keep sparks from flying into dry tinder. Everyone knows that campfires cause many forest and brush fires each year, some deadly.

Successfully cooking in Dutch Ovens fueled with campfire coals is nothing new. Our forefathers did it daily. With a little practice it is easily mastered; you just have to spend a little time serving your apprenticeship.

BEAN HOLE COOKING
CHAPTER TEN

A favorite method of baking in many remote hunting and fishing camps the United States and Canada is what is commonly called bean hole baking. Bean hole baking, according to historians, dates back for centuries to the early days of the Penobscot Indians of Maine. They found they could slow cook food by placing it in a hole dug in the earth that had been heated by a fire in the hole. They placed their food in the hole and covered it with rocks and earth to seal in the heat. At the end of the day they returned to uncover the hole, exposing the cooked food. America's first slow cooker was born.

Retrieving a Dutch Oven from a permanent bean hole in Alabama.

Early settlers learned this method of cooking in a hole in the ground and added the cast iron Dutch Oven as the vessel to hold the food. French fur traders carried this cooking technique into the Canadian northwest, mountain men took it to the Rockies, and explorers took it to other parts of North America.

This method of baking in a hole in the ground has survived several hundred years of improvements in stoves, ovens, and baking techniques. Back before gas and electric stoves were common, miners, logging camp cooks, remote resort lodge cooks, hunting and fishing camp cooks, and homestead cooks did much of their baking in cast iron Dutch Ovens in a hole filled with hot coals and covered with dirt. Because beans were the most common dish baked, *bean hole baking* became the name of this technique.

Early American outdoor writer Horace Kephart, writing in his 1906 best-selling book *Camping and Woodcraft*, called the bean hole a "bake-hole." He wrote, "Every fixed camp that has no stove should have a bake-hole, if for nothing else than baking beans." He continued, "The hole can be dug anywhere, but it is best in the side of a

A hot fire is built in the bean hole to heat the sides and bottom to cooking temperature.

Once the bean hole is heated, the Dutch Oven dish to be cooked is lowered into the hole. The bean hole is covered with dirt and left for hours as the food slowly bakes.

The moment of truth as the meal is uncovered.

bank or knoll, so that an opening can be left in front to rake out of, and for drainage in case of rain. Line it with stones, as they hold heat and keep the sides from crumbling. Have the completed hole a little larger than your baking kettle. Build a hardwood fire in and above the hole and keep it going until the stones or earth is very hot (not less than half an hour). Rake out most of the coals and ashes, put in the Dutch Oven, which must have a tight-fitting lid, cover with ashes and then with live coals; and, if a long heating is required, keep a small fire going on top. Close the mouth of the oven with a flat rock. This is the way for beans or braising meat."

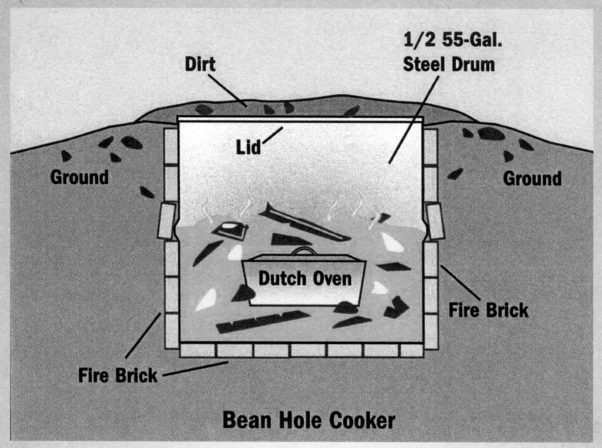

Bean hole plan.

BUILD A PERMANENT BEAN HOLE

I built a permanent bean hole at my camp at the base of Tater Knob Mountain in the Cumberland Mountains. Here is how you can build your own permanent bean hole.

Take a clean 55-gallon drum and cut it in half. Save the lid and discard the upper half. In a safe area, outside your cabin or camp, dig a hole a little deeper and wider than the half drum. Line the bottom and side of the hole with firebricks. Next, drill several small holes in the bottom of the drum to allow water to drain in the event water should ever get inside. Place about 3 inches of

Building a permanent bean hole is an easy DIY project.

sand in the bottom of the drum to prevent it from burning out. Put the drum in the firebrick-lined hole and fill in the spaces between the bricks and between the bricks and drum with sand. Place the lid on top of the drum and you have a permanent bean hole.

When you want to bake a pot of beans or any other dish, simply build a fire in the bean hole and let it burn hot for about 45 minutes. Remember, you are heating up the firebricks and soil next to the hole. When a hot bed of coals are ready, take a shovel and remove half of them from the bean hole. Next, place a cast iron Dutch Oven filled with beans or other dishes into the bed of coals in the bean hole, then put a couple shovelfuls of hot coals on top of the Dutch Oven. Put the cover on top of the drum and cover with dirt or sand. This will smother out the fire but will keep the temperature even for a long period of time. Go hiking or fishing for the day and return to a hot meal. As with most methods of cooking, it will take a few trials to perfect the method, but it is fun, and once it's worked out it will become a favorite method of baking in your camp.

CLEANING AND MAINTAINING YOUR DUTCH OVEN
CHAPTER ELEVEN

I t comes as a surprise to most first-time cast iron Dutch Oven cooks how easy it is to clean their seasoned ovens. It is much easier to clean a seasoned Dutch Oven than it is to scrub most conventional cooking pots and pans. In fact, it's possible to over-clean your Dutch Oven. The result is an oven that needs to be reseasoned.

Properly cleaning and maintaining your Dutch Oven is essential.

Cleaning the cast iron Dutch Oven is a three-step process:

1. REMOVE FOOD:

Using a wooden scraper, stainless steel CM scrubber, or plastic scraper, remove all of the food. *Never* use a metal scraper such as a spatula or steel wool/wire scouring pad and *never* wash in a dishwasher, as this will ruin the pot's seasoning.

Many Dutch Oven cooks say never to wash a seasoned oven and lid with soap, as it will ruin the seasoning and give the food cooked in the oven a soapy taste. I have found that a *well-seasoned* oven can be washed with warm water and a *mild* dishwashing soap without negative results. Be sure to rinse well with warm water.

If you have cooked something that has stuck to the oven and is difficult to remove, partially fill it with clean, warm water and bring to a boil. Brush carefully while boiling. Most stuck-on food will release when boiled. If not, scrub with a plastic scouring pad or plastic bristle brush. Never pour cold water into a hot oven, or hot water into a cold oven, as it can cause permanent damage to the oven. I once saw a cook cleaning a very hot oven pour cold water into it and the pot cracked. It was ruined.

Once all food is out of the oven and off the underside of the lid, rinse the pot and lid in warm water.

Care should be used in cleaning a seasoned cast iron pan. Use only a scrub pad or soft brush, like the one pictured below.

2. DRY:

Immediately after the oven has been rinsed, dry the entire oven and lid using a paper towel or clean cloth towel. Many cooks dry their ovens by placing them on heat until they are hot to the touch. The point is, you want your oven as dry as possible to prevent rust.

Once the oven and lid are dry, you will want to oil them lightly for long-term protection from rust.

3. OIL:

Coat the entire oven and lid, inside and out, with a light coat of vegetable or mineral oil. Be careful not to get the oil coating too thick as it will become a gummy mess in time. Also, a thick coating of oil will go bad quickly. Do not use lard for oiling, as it will turn rancid in a short period of time. In fact, most oils will go bad during periods of long storage, especially if the oven is stored with the lid on tight. Food cooked in a rancid pot will taste like the pot smells. I like to use mineral oil for long-term storage, as I have never had it turn rancid when my ovens were properly stored.

Dutch Ovens should be cleaned as quickly as possible after cooking a dish in them—the sooner the better. Never use a Dutch Oven for storing food, as the acid in foods will quickly penetrate the seasoning on the utensil, allowing the cast iron to come in direct contact with water and thus rust will appear when washed and dried. Never allow your oven to sit in water or water to stand on it. A cast iron Dutch Oven will rust before your eyes if you don't protect it from moisture.

Caution: I know people who have taken Dutch Ovens that have a lot of food stuck on them, or unknown gunk in the case of a Dutch Oven bought secondhand, and placed them in their self-cleaning kitchen oven. Sometimes it worked, but I have heard of the gunk catching on fire and, since the oven is on self-clean mode, the door is locked. The results are a potential house fire. For this reason, I do not recommend using the high heat of a self-cleaning oven to clean Dutch Ovens. The boiling method, as previously mentioned, is far safer.

STORAGE

Since most Dutch Ovens go for long periods without use, proper storage techniques are important for the oven to protect it from rusting or turning rancid.

First, select a place to store your ovens that is protected from moisture and dust. Where I live in the South, a Dutch Oven stored in an enclosed garage or outside storage room will be subject to rusting rapidly due to our high humidity. I like to store my Dutch Ovens in the family room as fireplace decorations. In the house, the central heat and air keeps the humidity under control.

Regardless of where you store your Dutch Ovens, *never* store them with the lid on tight. That will almost guarantee moisture condensing on the inside and rusting the pot. Also, the lack of air movement will cause most oil coatings to turn rancid.

To properly store your Dutch Oven, place the lid on the pot using a spacer to keep the lid ajar to allow air movement. A couple sheets of paper towels rolled up can serve this purpose. Some people use a small roll of aluminum foil as a spacer. You want a good exchange of air from the inside of the pot to the outside.

Some people go one step further and place a piece of real charcoal, not charcoal briquette, wrapped up in a paper towel. This absorbs odor and moisture.

DEALING WITH RUST

Rust is an enemy of cast iron, and even the most well cared for Dutch Ovens can develop rust spots. The first rule in dealing with rust is to examine your oven regularly for it. Be sure to look inside and out and examine the lid thoroughly. The sooner you find rust, the better. Over a period of time, rust can ruin the oven, and it can happen quicker than you might believe.

When rust is found on your Dutch Oven, you should deal with it immediately. First, remove the rust with a wire brush or steel wool.

Once the rust has been removed, it will be necessary to reseason your Dutch Oven.

RESEASONING AN OVEN

One of the major reasons cast iron Dutch Ovens need to be reseasoned is that they are improperly cleaned. Harsh detergents and scrubbings with metal scrapers can do damage to an oven's seasoning.

Other reasons Dutch Ovens need to be reseasoned is if they have become rusted or are improperly stored and the oil turns rancid. Regardless of the reason, it's essential to ensure your cast iron Dutch Oven is properly seasoned. For instructions, visit the use and care section at www.lodgemfg.com.

Compare the color of the unseasoned oven on the left to the seasoned oven on the right.

TRANSPORTING A DUTCH OVEN

Dutch Ovens have a way of traveling a lot. It may be to a friend's house for a backyard cookout, on a family camping trip, in the RV, on a canoe trip, or to the family cabin. Regardless of where it is going, the oven needs to be packed for the trip in a way that the oven is protected and those items it comes in contact with are also protected. I was once on a canoe trip where an improperly packed Dutch Oven leg went through the canvas canoe bottom, causing a major leak. I have seen Dutch Ovens unloaded from a vehicle dropped on concrete and broken. I have seen them hit lantern globes in an SUV cargo area and break the glass.

Transporting a Dutch Oven is best done with a heavy-duty carrying case designed for Dutch Ovens.

Many Dutch Oven cooks purchase specially designed padded Dutch Oven transporting bags, such as the Camp Gourmet Dutch Oven Case available from GSI, the Dutch Oven bag from Chuckwagon Supply, or the Camp Dutch Oven Tote Bag from Lodge Manufacturing Company. These are a good investment if your Dutch Oven is going to be transported.

CHAPTER TWELVE

With the many wonderful accessories available today, even the new Dutch Oven cook can start out cooking like an expert.

They allow you to get a fire going quickly, handle the ovens safely, control the fire with ease, cook at a comfortable height, check temperatures, and keep the oven clean. What our ancestors would have given for these accessories.

COOKING TABLE

Today, Dutch Oven cooking is being done as often in backyards and parks as in the backcountry and around campfires. Most of it is done using charcoal briquettes rather than coals from an open fire. To accommodate cooks using charcoal, someone came up with the idea of having a steel table upon which to cook. It put the ovens at a comfortable height, which made cooking much easier when compared to bending over ovens on the ground. The table made it easy to position the charcoal briquettes and was easy to clean after use. Also, the table saved yards and parks from having burn spots where charcoal was placed for ground cooking.

As the cooking table continued to evolve, innovations were added to make the table more user-friendly. Removable wind screens were added, which helped make cooking time somewhat predictable on cold or windy days. Then someone came up with folding legs, which made the table easy to store and pack. Adjustable legs were added, which made the table adjustable for uneven cooking sites.

The cooking table I use, the Camp Dutch Oven Cooking Table made by Lodge Manufacturing Company, has all of these features. It is all steel construction, weighs 34 pounds, folds flat for easy carrying and storage, and can be erected within a minute or so. The table top measures 32 inches by 16 inches and is 26

A long-handled shovel keeps your hands away from the heat.

Dutch Oven cooking table.

inches tall and can accommodate two to four Dutch Ovens, depending on the sizes being used and whether stack cooking is being done.

Other companies that offer Dutch Oven cooking tables include Cabela's and Chuckwagon Supply.

Keep a whisk broom and scraper, such as a putty knife, with the table to help with the table cleanup.

CHARCOAL CHIMNEY STARTER

I wish I had known about the charcoal chimney starter many years ago. It saves a lot of time getting charcoal to a cooking temperature and does not require starter fuel. It is simply a metal chimney in which the charcoal briquettes are stacked. A sheet or two of newspaper is wadded up in the bottom and set on fire. In just a few minutes, you have briquettes ready to set under and on top of your Dutch Oven. I see these inexpensive starters for sale in home improvement stores and Lodge Manufacturing Company has them.

This straight-sided aluminum pan is designed to fit inside a Dutch Oven.

CAKE RACKS AND PIZZA PANS

During my early days of Dutch Oven cooking, I was like many beginners, and I was still burning some dishes no matter how hard I tried to master cooking in the black pot.

This all changed when I was on a hunt in a remote camp in Montana where the camp cook used cake racks and heavy-duty aluminum straight-sided pans in his Dutch Ovens and simply used the ovens like an oven at home. Since the 2- to 3-inch-deep pans containing food sat on top of the racks, no food was burned. The racks allowed for good air circulation and eliminated hot spots. The heavy-duty aluminum pans kept the food away from the oven so cleanup was a snap.

When I returned home, I went to a restaurant supply store and purchased cake racks and heavy-duty American Metalcraft aluminum straight-sided pans to fit inside each of my ovens. (NOTE: Many Dutch Oven cooks use these pans and call them cake pans, but at restaurant supply stores and mail-order houses they are called pizza pans.) You will want to get pans that are smaller in diameter than your Dutch Oven. For example, for your 12-inch oven you will want to get a 10-inch or 9-inch pan. The smaller diameter pan gives you room for the pan lifter to grip the pan for removal from a hot oven. Also, make sure to get a pan that has short enough sides so your Dutch Oven lid will fit in place properly. You don't want the lid to be lifted and riding on the pan rim. A cake pan with a depth of 2 to 3 inches is typically safe for this purpose.

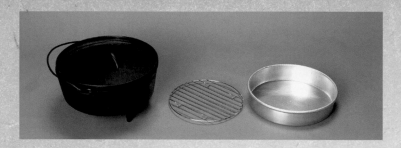

Dutch Oven with cake rack and heavy-duty aluminum pan.

I also purchased a heavy-duty, professional-size pan lifter that makes lifting an aluminum pan of food out of a hot oven easy. It is almost impossible to remove a hot pan of food from a hot Dutch Oven without the lifter.

I now use this cake rack/pan combination for many recipes in all of my ovens, and it has cut down on much of the work I used to do when Dutch Oven cooking. By using the aluminum pans, I don't have to worry cooking beans or dishes with high acid content like tomatoes. I also use it with dishes that have a lot of sugar in them to help with the cleanup. Other than an occasional spillover, the food never touches the cast iron. I am now seeing more chuckwagon cooks use this method of cooking, and with good reason.

Also, I have added several loft pans to my outfit. I can cook two dishes at once by using two loft pans, on a cake rack, in my larger ovens. And they are nice for dishes like meatloaf and cobbler. For specialty dishes such as pineapple upside down cake, I have an aluminum pan designed for that dish.

American Metalcraft and other brands of heavy-duty aluminum round pizza pans can be found at many sources by doing a search on the Internet. Most restaurant supply dealers also have them. The same supplier should have cake racks and pot lifters, as well.

The inverted lid of a Dutch Oven can be used as a skillet when set on a lid holder and hot coals are placed under the lid.

Parchment papers, made for Dutch Ovens, make good liners for baking.

If you want a heavy-duty rack to put in your oven, say to cook a large cut of meat, then you will want to get the round cast iron trivet/meat rack from Lodge. Not only is it a good rack to use in your oven, it can also serve as a heavy-duty trivet to place hot dishes on when setting up a serving line.

The downside to using cake pans in your Dutch Ovens is that it will cut down on the amount of food you can cook at one time when compared to filling an oven without a cake rack and pan. I don't always use cake pans; there are many dishes that I like to cook in a bare oven.

ALUMINUM FOIL PANS AND PARCHMENT PAPER DUTCH OVEN LINERS

If you don't want to use a cake pan, then you can use aluminum foil or parchment liners. I have used both with satisfaction. Every year I am part of a chuckwagon team that cooks for an outdoor expo. We cook enough peach cobbler to serve more than six hundred people in one afternoon. For this event we usually have twenty Dutch Ovens going all afternoon. To speed up the process, we use cast iron trivets and aluminum foil pans in our ovens. The disposable foil pans keep the ovens clean and go straight from the hot oven to the serving table.

Parchment paper liners, usually used for baking pies and cakes, are compact to pack, keep the oven clean, and after use are 100 percent biodegradable. Removing food in parchment paper from the hot oven can be a little tricky, but with a little experience it can be done easily. The parchment paper liners offered by Lodge are made to fit Dutch Ovens.

Scrapers suitable for cast iron Dutch Ovens

SCRAPERS

Food stuffs burn and stick to the inside of Dutch Ovens. This is a common occurrence if you cook much at all. When washing the oven there is a tendency to scrape off the stuck-on food with a metal spatula or with steel wool. Don't! These will take the seasoning off the pot and will require you to reseason the oven. To scrub out cast iron pots I like to keep the following tools on hand:

1. Earlywood tera scraper, a heavy-duty wooden scraper made specifically for cast iron.
2. An interesting 4-inch square pad of stainless steel chain mail (linked rings) called the Knapp Made CM Scrubber. This handy little scrubber will not rub off the seasoning, is easy to use, and will last a lifetime.
3. A Lodge plastic pan scraper.

Each of these makes cleaning off stuck/burned-on food quick and easy and will not destroy the oven's seasoning.

LID LIFTER

The lid lifter is a combination tool. It enables the cook to lift a hot and heavy Dutch Oven lid with hot ashes on it without it swinging. Also, it enables the cook to lift the entire oven by catching the wire bail and pulling the oven up. This is a valuable tool, as it will also be used to rotate the Dutch Oven lid during the cooking process.

Lid lifters may be purchased in a variety of lengths and designs, from a simple couple of hooks on a steel rod to a deluxe model that allows the cook to tighten the hold on the Dutch Oven lid

Basic lid lifter.

using a grip. This is one of the Dutch Oven cook's most valuable tools, and it is usually available where Dutch Ovens are sold. Take the time to try out different types. Find the one that allows you to lift heavy lids safely and with ease.

LID STAND

The lid stand is made from heavy bar stock steel. It is designed to give the cook a clean stand upon which to place the Dutch Oven lid when opening the Dutch Oven. A great second use of the lid stand is to put hot charcoal briquettes around the stand and place a Dutch Oven lid upside down on the stand to use as a griddle. Frying eggs, meats, or fish on the inverted lid is just as easy as using a frying pan. It works really well on a steel cooking table. A third use of the lid stand is preheating the lid for recipes that call for a preheated oven. Place a few coals under the lid stand and place the lid on it, and in just a few minutes you have a preheated lid.

Deluxe lid lifter in use.

Lid stand

LONG-HANDLED TONGS

To accurately and safely place and move hot charcoal briquettes, I like to use stainless steel tongs that have long handles. The ones I like have 16-inch handles and make placing briquettes quick and easy. They are also good for moving food around in a hot oven. I keep two tongs in my cook outfit, one for moving briquettes and one for food. They are sold at most places that sell Dutch Ovens. I like the ones with wood inserts in the handles; they are much easier and cooler on the hands.

Long-handled tongs in use.

HEAVY LEATHER GLOVES

Almost everything you touch when Dutch Oven cooking is hot, and splashing hot liquids comes with the territory. To prevent burns, a pair of wielders gloves or heavy-duty leather gloves made for Dutch Oven cooking should be available to the cook. The gloves I use are designed for Dutch Oven cooking and are sold by Lodge Manufacturing Company. They have saved my hands from many unnecessary burns.

TRIPOD

If your Dutch Oven cooking involves cooking over a campfire, then you will want to have a sturdy tripod as a part of your gear. I like the tripods whose legs are interlocked at the top and with a hook that holds an adjustable chain for hooking to the Dutch Ovens wire bail. You can get them

Heavy leather gloves

in various leg lengths; however, I prefer a tripod with 60-inch legs to give me more room for cooking over a campfire. Don't settle for a tripod made from anything less than ½-inch bar stock. There is a lot of weight suspended over a fire when you are cooking in a cast iron Dutch Oven filled with hot oil or stew. That is the wrong time to find out the tripod you are using is weak. Tripods designed for this use come with one-piece legs or with legs that unscrew for easy packing. I use a tripod sold by Lodge Manufacturing Company. They are also available from Chuckwagon Supply and Cabela's.

Tripod in use.

SHOVELS

Using coals from a campfire to heat Dutch Ovens requires the use of a long-handled shovel. I have used short-handled shovels, such as the military entrenching tool, on canoe or horseback trips, but they put your hands uncomfortably close to the fire. Most cooks depend on the standard pointed or square-point shovel available at any hardware store. I have one of each in my cooking gear. The serious Dutch Oven cook may drill several ¾-inch holes in the shovel so that all small coals and ashes can be shaken out in the fire, delivering the larger, more desirable coals to the Dutch Oven. I use a small fireplace shovel when I clean my steel cooking table.

Long-handled shovels

WHISK BROOM

Dutch Oven cooking involves the use of coals on the lid of the vessel, and sometime during the cooking process you will need to either remove the ashes or add more coals. It's especially important at the end so ashes don't get into the food when the lid is removed. A small whisk broom,

Whisk broom

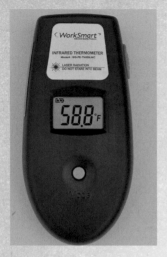

58.8°F

Laser thermometer

such as those sold for automobile clean-up, is ideal for this purpose. It can also be a handy tool to use in cleaning the steel cooking table.

THERMOMETERS

While you won't look like a mountain man, you can get a temperature reading on your Dutch Ovens from a safe distance with an infrared laser thermometer. It can be a great way to learn just how many coals you need, under specific conditions, to have your oven reach a certain temperature. By using one, I have learned just how much difference the wind, outside temperature, type and number of coals, etc., can make in having a constant oven temperature. The infrared laser thermometer can take a lot of guesswork out of keeping the oven at the temperature you want.

Also, I keep a digital meat thermometer on hand to determine when meats reach the internal temperature I want.

WOODEN UTENSILS

One or more long handle large wooden spoons are essential for Dutch Oven cooking. They are soft and will not hurt the patina, and they don't burn the mouth when taste testing. Besides, this was the traditional spoon that was used with the first Dutch Ovens. Dutch Oven master chef George Precter would not look like himself if he did not have a wooden spoon in his hand when cooking; it is his trademark. He is well known for using the spoon to adjust a Dutch Oven hanging by its bail over an open fire. Also, he frequently taps the lids of Dutch Ovens cooking in coals. No one knows what he hears when he does that. And he swears by the wooden spoon when stirring or sampling a dish.

Wooden utensils are ideal for Dutch Oven cooking.

I also like to use a wooden scraper when cleaning a Dutch Oven, as it will not damage the seasoning of the oven.

A good source of high-quality, long lasting wooden utensils are those made by Brad Bernhart of Earlywood Designs in Red Lodge, Montana. They are the ones I use. Their address is given in the appendix of this book. I use two of his spoons made of jatoba and two scrapers—one made of ebony and one made of jatoba. These woods are dense and strong and with care will last many years of hard use. Also, they are very good looking even after hard use.

CARE OF YOUR WOODEN UTENSILS

Here is how Brad Bernhart recommends you get the most out of your wooden spoons, scrapers, etc.

GENERAL TIPS

The first thing to remember is that water is not a friend of wood. It can cause your utensils to swell, warp, fade, and crack. To prevent this, handwash your utensils with hot soapy water and dry in a rack. The wash cycles in a dishwasher are too long, and those high-temp drying cycles don't help either. They soak up water and dry out but don't get scrubbed. This will make your utensils turn gray, fuzzy, and have a short life.

SCRUBBING

After the first few times you used your utensils, you may have noticed your spoons looking or feeling a little fuzzy. That's to be expected, as the grain of the wood is raised by exposure to water. If that hasn't worn off by now, rub your utensils with a Scotch-Brite pad. Use the little purple one

Mineral oil gives wooden utensils a long life.

you got with your purchase or the scratchy green side of your dish sponge. A one-time scrub will remove the fuzz for life. Keep the pad; it can be used again and again on your other wooden items.

OIL

Every once in a while, give your utensils a good coat of oil. We prefer mineral oil because it is food safe, has no scent, never goes rancid, and soaks in quickly. The oil will repel water and thus reduce the number of times your utensils go through the wet/dry cycle. This will prevent warping, fading, and cracking that can be caused by repeated exposure to water. Give them every bit of oil and they will soak it up. It's a good idea to put on as much as you can, then let them sit overnight before drying any extra off with a towel. Check out our very own Earlywood Oil, which works excellent on hardwoods and has a hint of lemon peel oil to kill bacteria, smell great, and help eliminate stubborn cutting board odors (like garlic or onions).

In my opinion, oiling wooden spoons is one of life's simple pleasures. It's akin to seasoning a Dutch Oven or waterproofing a good pair of hiking boots or leather gloves. Take your time and enjoy it! If you want to keep your Earlywood utensils in like-new condition, oil them every five to six uses, but if you're a fan of that well-used look (like we are), then you can oil them every three to six months.

ACCESSORIES

I have found that since I am serving many meals in outdoor settings, I need a set of enamel plates, bowls, and cups. I use the blue and red enamelware made by the Coleman Company. They are tough and look good when the table is set. For flatware, I have come to depend upon sporks made by Light My Fire. This clever all-in-one eating utensil has a fork on one end and a spoon on the other with a cutting edge. They are tough and come in a variety of colors.

Also, you will need a variety of mixing bowls, measuring cup, set of measuring spoons, and cooking knives.

As you get more into Dutch Oven cooking, you will find your own favorite set of accessories that makes your cooking more fun and less work.

A BRIEF HISTORY OF THE DUTCH OVEN
CHAPTER THIRTEEN

O*ne of the most often-stated reasons Dutch Oven cooking enthusiasts give for using the vessel is that it puts them in touch with the past; it has a bit of history associated with it. I have to agree, for, as I cook in my Dutch Ovens, I am reminded of the explorers, settlers, long-hunters, mountain men, and chuckwagon cooks who mastered the oven long before I came along.*

EARLY HISTORY OF CAST IRON COOKING POTS

The earliest reference I can find about cast-iron cooking vessels is from the seventh century. Later, during the reign of Edward III, in the 1300s, iron cooking pots and skillets were considered part of the Crown Jewels.

While we don't know for sure that Columbus used cast iron cooking pots on his trips to the New World, we do know that ships at that time used iron kettles to cook meals. They had sandboxes where the cook built a fire and, during calm seas, meals were cooked in the kettles hung over the fires. There is some reference to the Pilgrims cooking in such a fashion when they came across the Atlantic to the New World. We do know that cast iron pots, usually referred to as kettles or cooking kettles, were made in America as early as 1650. Cast-aluminum Dutch Ovens didn't appear until about 1889.

THE EMERGENCE OF THE DUTCH OVEN WE KNOW TODAY

As the explorers and settlers pushed over the mountains, they carried their iron cookware with them.

Dutch Ovens as we know them today were developing in the early eighteenth century. The use of heavy cast iron cookware was highly regarded in Europe, as they allowed heat to be evenly distributed through the pot. There was also a rapidly growing demand for cast iron cooking pots in America. The iron stove had not been invented and most cooking was done on fireplace hearths, outdoors over campfires, or over open fires in lean-tos behind homes. A cast iron pot was emerging that was ideal for this type of cooking. It was flat on the bottom, had three legs to hold the pot's bottom above hot coals, and had a flat lid upon which to place hot coals for baking. Paul Revere has been credited by some writers with making many of the improvements to the early oven. The Dutch Oven as we know it today was being created.

THE ORIGIN OF ITS NAME

No one knows for sure where the name Dutch Oven came from. Perhaps the most plausible explanation, as is reported in John Ragsdale's book *Dutch Ovens Chronicled*, is that in 1704 Englishman foundry owner Abraham Darby traveled to Holland to inspect casting of some brass vessels in dry sand molds. Holland had more advanced foundry technology, and many thick-walled, heavy cast iron vessels were imported into Britain. From this observation, and after some experiments, Darby perfected a method to cast iron vessels in dry sand molds. In 1708, he patented the process and soon produced a large number of cooking pots. By the mid-eighteenth century, these pots were being shipped to the Colonies. They were first referred to as Dutch pots, later Dutch Ovens.

Another explanation is that once the improved cast iron cooking pot became popular in America, British and New England manufacturers produced it in large numbers. Dutch traders traveled throughout the American colonies and frontier and peddled the pots, thus the name Dutch Ovens.

There are several other theories as to how the name came about; however, we will never know for sure. The one thing that is for sure is the name stuck and has been in use for almost three centuries.

OVER THE MOUNTAINS

The Dutch Oven was a much needed and valued part of the homestead as pioneers moved toward the Appalachian Mountains. As longhunters explored the wilderness areas "over the mountains," they carried the Dutch Oven to use in their base camps. In her book *Seedtime on the Cumberland*, historian Harriette Simpson Arnow tells about longhunters in 1769 not having a Dutch Oven large enough to cook a forty-pound wild turkey.

The Dutch Ovens we use today evolved from cast iron cookware depended on by early Americans. Entire meals were cooked on the fireplace hearth and the cast iron Dutch Oven was the main cooking vessel.

LEWIS AND CLARK

In 1804, one of the greatest expeditions in history departed St. Louis to explore the United States' newly acquired Louisiana Territory. The Lewis and Clark Expedition was to be one of the most famous camping trips of all time. The cast iron Dutch Oven would certainly be one of the choice cooking vessels of the expedition, or would it?

After researching published journals of the expedition written by Lewis as well as by expedition member Patrick Gass, I then obtained a list of the supplies Lewis purchased, but there was never any mention of cast iron Dutch Ovens.

In 2003, I attended a lecture by Professor Gary E. Moulton of the University of Nebraska. Dr. Moulton is a Lewis and Clark Expedition scholar. At the end of the lecture, I told Dr. Moulton the problems I was having with my research. He smiled and said, "Read the journal expedition member Joseph Whitehouse kept and you will find the proof you need."

Whitehouse writes of caching Dutch Ovens on Tuesday, June 11, 1805. There you have it, from someone who was there; the Lewis and Clark Expedition did have Dutch Ovens on the trip.

MOUNTAIN MEN AND DUTCH OVENS

Soon to follow Lewis and Clark were the mountain men. In their quest for beaver, they went into remote regions of the west where no Europeans had gone before.

There is enough recorded about their camps and activities to prove the Dutch Oven was an important part of their base camps. Mountain man Osborne Russell wrote in April 1834 that their "camp kettles had not been greased for some time."

To many adventurers exploring the Louisiana Purchase, the Dutch Oven was their kitchen.

In Don Holm's book *Old-Fashioned Dutch Oven Cookbook*, he tells about John Colter, one of the members of the Lewis and Clark Expedition who became a mountain man, dying in 1813. Colter's Dutch Oven was sold for the equivalent of a weeks' pay, $4, at the executor's auction. He kept his Dutch Oven to the end.

Cast iron Dutch Ovens, favored by mountainmen and Indians alike for cooking, were one of the more popular trade items at the annual fur trade rendezvous.

WESTERN SETTLERS

There are many accounts of Dutch Ovens being listed as necessary items for settlers moving west to have if they were to join a wagon

BELOW: Mountain men of the early 1800s used Dutch Ovens in their base camps, and they were popular trade goods at their annual rendezvous.

The first settlers in the Appalachian Mountains had no stoves, only their fireplaces and Dutch Ovens and/or iron skillets.

train. The black pot was a favorite among the Mormons as they made their way to the Great Salt Lake. Utah history recorded that the miners digging in the canyons around Bingham, Price, and Cedar City counted on the black pots and valued them as essential as their picks.

Remote homesteaders and ranchers only had the home fireplace in which to cook, and cast iron Dutch Ovens and skillets were considered some of their most valuable furnishings. Where wood was scarce, dried buffalo dung or dried cow dung was used as a fuel source.

COWBOYS, CHUCKWAGONS, AND DUTCH OVENS

Perhaps nowhere in history did the cast iron Dutch Oven play a larger role in feeding hungry workers than in the cow camps of the American west. Chuckwagon cooks demanded their outfits include several Dutch Ovens. (It's still that way today.) All you have to do to see this in action is to look at the many paintings by Charles Russell and Frederic Remington of cow camps.

DUTCH OVENS WENT TO WAR

The Dutch Oven was a part of cooking gear for many soldiers on both sides of the War Between the States. Rations of beans and cornmeal were quickly turned into a tasty meal using the Dutch Oven. The oven could also turn local crops, such as corn, peanuts, and turnip greens, into a hot meal when they were on "short rations."

JOSEPH LODGE BUILDS CAST IRON FOUNDRY

In 1896, Pennsylvanian Joseph Lodge built a cast iron foundry in the Cumberland Plateau foothills town of South Pittsburg, Tennessee. One of its best known products was Dutch Ovens. It is now one of the most modern cast iron cookware foundries in the world, the leading producer of cast

Chuckwagon cooks have used Dutch Ovens as essential parts of their cooking outfits since the beginning of the U.S. cattle industry.

iron Dutch Ovens worldwide, and the only one remaining in the United States.

COOKING VESSEL OF CHOICE IN EARLY 1900s WORKING CAMPS

As America grew following the First World War, working camps sprung up in remote areas of North America. Mining, logging, trapping, etc., put men and women into locations where iron stoves were impractical to have and the cast iron Dutch Oven was depended on to feed the hungry workers.

SCOUTS CONTINUE THE TRADITION

As wood-burning stoves became popular, followed by modern gas and electric ranges, the Dutch Oven began to fade away as a relic of the past. Fortunately for us, the Boy Scout and Girl Scout organizations recognized the value of Dutch Oven cooking as part of their camping programs and kept the art of Dutch Oven cooking alive. Some of the best Dutch Oven cooking tips and techniques available today come from the scouts and their leaders.

COOK-OFFS AND GATHERINGS REKINDLE DUTCH OVEN COOKING

In the late 1970s and early 1980s, various cook-offs were becoming popular. Some were chuckwagon cooking competitions, others wild game or chili cook-offs. The one thing that was common among many of the cook-offs was the use of the cast iron Dutch Oven. Soon Dutch Oven cooking became a popular means of cooking at home or in a campground.

Dutch Oven cooking became so popular that in 1984 the International Dutch Oven Society (IDOS) was formed. The organization was started after the Great American Dutch Oven Cook-off

Today, delicious meals can be easily prepared in Dutch Ovens on patios and in parks just as our forefathers did in their cabins and camps.

in Logan, Utah, had been held for five years with great success. Today, the IDOS has members from all over the United States and several countries.

Interest in Dutch Oven cooking is worldwide and there have been Dutch Oven societies and gatherings organized in other countries such as the Japan Dutch Oven Society (JDOS) and Camp Oven Cooking in Australia (COCIA).

OFFICIAL COOK POT OF UTAH

The people of the state of Utah think so much of the Dutch Oven and the tradition of cooking in this black pot that in 1997 the state legislature enacted legislation designating the Dutch Oven as the state's cooking pot. Utah is the number one market for Dutch Ovens.

Dutch Oven cooking is being discovered by an ever increasing number of outdoor cooks. It is a fun and delicious way to cook almost any dish, and it has a touch of history that adds spice to the meal.

APPENDIX

U.S. MADE DUTCH OVEN & ACCESSORY SOURCES

Dutch Oven Manufacturers

CAST IRON

Lodge Manufacturing
Company
www.lodgemfg.com

ALUMINUM

GSI Outdoors
www.gsioutdoors.com

Mail-order Supplies

Chuckwagon Supply Company
www.chuckwagonsupply.com

Cabela's
www.cabelas.com

Camp Chef
www.campchef.com

Charcoal

Kingsford Products Company
www.kingsford.com

Dutch Oven Societies

International Dutch Oven
Society (IDOS)
www.idos.com

Japan Dutch Oven Society (JDOS)
www.jdos.com

Camp Oven Cooking in
Australia (COCIA)
www.aussiecampovencook.com

Wooden Cooking Utensils

Earlywood Designs
www.earlywooddesigns.com

Pizza Pans and Cake Racks

American Metalcraft
www.amnow.com

Campware

The Coleman Company
www.coleman.com

Stainless Steel Scrubber

KnappMade CM Scrubber
www.cmscrubber.com

Sporks

Light My Fire, Inc.
www.lightmyfire.com

Gravy and Mixes

Pioneer Brand
www.pioneerbrand.com

Fire Rings

Pilot Rock Fire Rings
www.pilotrock.com

INDEX